FLYING DEATH

THE VIETNAM EXPERIENCE

by

SAMUEL K. BEAMON

Bloomington, IN   Milton Keynes, UK

authorHOUSE

AuthorHouse™
1663 Liberty Drive, Suite 200
Bloomington, IN 47403
www.authorhouse.com
Phone: 1-800-839-8640

AuthorHouse™ *UK Ltd.*
500 Avebury Boulevard
Central Milton Keynes, MK9 2BE
www.authorhouse.co.uk
Phone: 08001974150

First published by AuthorHouse 5/24/2007

ISBN: 978-1-4140-8302-5 (e)
ISBN: 978-1-4140-8301-8 (sc)
ISBN: 978-1-4140-8300-1 (hc)

Library of Congress Control Number: 2007902508
Printed in the United States of America
Bloomington, Indiana

This book is printed on acid-free paper.

Cover Picture Design by Ken Foran

I dedicate this book,

To my Parents, who were much smarter and wiser far beyond their years.

To all of those that served this country in the military, especially in the country of South Vietnam.

To all those that fought the War of Equality, to make this land a better place to live.

All of their sacrifices will never be forgotten.

CONTENTS

PREFACE

I have written this story about some of the things that I remember, during a short period of my life. These memories happened so very long ago, but had a profound influence on my life. They are some of the people and events that have guided me. These memories gave me the strength that allowed me to face my fears, to develop my aspirations and pursue my dreams.

There are certain things which occur in your life that will define you as a person. It might be the influence of your family or your environment. What makes an individual do certain things in their life? It is the pride in who you are, what you have learned, respect for your ancestors, and parents. They were the ones that tried to show you what was expected from you, along with the education you received and the church that you attended. These are all the cornerstones of your personality and character.

Nobody said that life was going to be easy or fair. The stories of what had been done to African Americans by other Americans, not only in the South but also in the North, have been well documented. The discrimination, segregation and unequal treatment is almost beyond belief. What does it take to be a member of this society? What does it take to be an American?

You never forget the past, to make the future better. Some countries have been around for thousands of years. The United States is only a baby compared with these countries. No other country has developed so far and in such a short span of time. This country has taken people from all around the world. Some people came here voluntarily, some were brought here to be slaves, while some were already here and nearly exterminated. They have taken the best and the worst of people to build a world power. In this land of freedom, how could they deny those same freedoms to some of its own citizens?

From the very beginning of this country, Blacks have served this country proudly. Fighting a war is very difficult, but fighting a war against your fellow citizens for your own inalienable rights is even harder. These are the same rights that the Constitution guarantees every citizen. They had fought against oppression around the world, only to come home, and face those same oppressions. In many cases, the treatment here was worse than what the evil tyrants were doing in other countries. Whether it was in the military or in civilian life, there was unequal treatment.

You do not change a person or a country's way of thinking by running away. You stand and fight against the injudicious and discriminatory treatment. This only makes the most oppressed people the strongest. They would have to fight for everything that they got and nothing would be given to them. Facing tremendous odds and many obstacles that were placed in front of them, they overcame. You can be anything that you want to be. Today is better than yesterday, but not as good as tomorrow. In the land of opportunity, dare to dream and be your own person. The doors of equal opportunity are open. The struggle for equality continues.

To this effort, I dedicate my story.

FORWARD

My parents were Milton and Mary Louise Beamon. During World War II, Mom worked in the factory like most people did. The people that were on the home front made the bullets, bombs, shell casings and anything else that was needed to win the war. Dad came home from the war and they were married on June 2, 1946. I was born Samuel Kenneth on July 27, 1947 and into the postwar generation known as the "Baby Boomers."

I was the oldest of their four boys and we lived in Waterbury, Connecticut. It was an industrial city, known as the Brass Capitol of the World. It is located in the middle of the state. We lived in the north end section of the city. My father, our neighbors, and relatives, all worked in the many brass mills. There were very few cars. The workers walked down the many hills to their jobs in the factories. At the end of their shifts, they were greasy, dirty and had to walk uphill to their homes. The neighborhood was that of a working class, which was consisted of French, Irish, Italian, Polish, Black and some Spanish. Nobody was "Rich" and everyone worked very hard for whatever they had. It was a true melting pot of different ethnic backgrounds. Everyone was treated equally. People were treated the way that they treated you. We were all the same and no one ever felt superior to anyone else. There was a true sense of an American Community.

First and foremost, it was important that we had a strong religious foundation. Each Sunday, my brothers and I were off to Sunday School and Church. My parents began the building of character in each of us at an early age. When we left the house, we carried the family name and we were responsible for the name. Be proud of who you are, stand tall, hold your head up, never look down and believe that you are somebody. Then came education, I went to Walsh Grammar School, which was predominately attended by White Students at the time.

As my brothers and I were getting older, we joined different youth organizations. We were all members of the Boys Club. Greg joined the Boy Scouts, Reggie was in the Junior Elks, and I was a member of the Sons of the American Legion. After a year, all four of us, including my youngest brother Milton had joined the Young Marine Program. Former Marines of the Brass City Memorial Detachment of the Marine Corps League founded this program in Waterbury. Within a few years, there were more than 300 children involved in the program. This program helped to set the standard for us to live by with pride in ones self and respect for others.

Growing up, we were also looking for heroes and role models, just like everyone else. I was like millions of kids and wanted to be like Davy Crockett, Superman or Mickey Mantle. There was very little said about Jessie Owens, Jackie Robinson, Willie Mays, or even Lena Horne. The achievements of these people and many more were whispered throughout the Negro community. It was like an untold history of this country. How can you be proud of who you are and where you are going, if you do not know where you came from?

Before graduating from grammar school, I tested to attend Kaynor Regional Vocational Technical High School and was accepted for enrollment. I had chosen this school, because at this time, college was not for me. This school was the same as to the racial makeup, very few Blacks. Both schools were the finest in the area. I always seemed to be in the minority, but it didn't bother me. Was I special? I didn't think I was, then again, everyone couldn't attend these schools. Graduation day from grammar school brought a special surprise. The American Legion had awarded me their Americanism Award.

Upon entering high school, I took the automobile mechanic course, in addition to the regular high school courses. Dad wasn't very happy and he didn't want me to be a knuckle busting, grease monkey mechanic. I was not the smartest person in the class and had to work hard for my grades. I learned that you can't gain anything without hard work and perseverance.

My parents believed in education. They would settle for nothing less than our graduating from school. We had learned in school about Slavery, Frederick Douglass, Booker T. Washington, and George Washington Carver. There was nothing taught about accomplishments of the Negro as to the history of this country, with the exception for slavery, picking cotton and peanuts. There was a time that it was illegal for a Negro to get an education in this country. This was not even mentioned in school. Negroes could sing and dance, but there were very few on television. As for Black actors and actresses, there were a few in the movies, but they played butlers and maids. Black Politicians were almost nonexistent. Where were our civic leaders? There was something wrong with this picture. What was the role of Negroes in this country? Where were our heroes? Every ethnic group has the right to know about their contributions to this country's history.

Growing up during this time was difficult. Mom and Dad always told us that we could be anything that we wanted to be. This was their challenge given to us and they had laid the ground work. It would be our responsibility to meet this challenge. Society had a different view of things. The White Majority stated that the Negro was not smart and could not operate complicated machinery, fly airplanes or take any type of leadership role. It was said that the Negroes did not have the brainpower to even be the quarterback a football team. They were not allowed on or even to play on golf courses or tennis courts. This was exactly opposite from what my parents had told us. For many years, there were White and Negro sport leagues. The color barrier was broken in sports. Negroes were now playing on the White teams. Opportunities in the business world were also being denied, not because of their lack of ability, but by the color of their skin. The races were being kept separate in everything that was being done in this country. This was reality and not what was being taught in school. All of this brought about more questions. Why was this being done? This was supposed to be the land of equal opportunity for its citizens. All of the American citizens were Americans or were they?

Who was right, My Parents or Society? My Parents never told me anything that wasn't good for me or for my own good. This Country and its Society were going to have to change not only its way of thinking, but also the way it was treating and looking at its citizens. All of its citizens!

HOME LIFE

Growing up during the 1950's and 1960's was a disturbing, confusing and an exciting time. I guess that the country was trying to find itself. There was so much going on. I had been taught to love and respect this country. My grandfather had been a veteran of World War One, while my father, uncles and cousins were veterans of World War Two. I also had an uncle and cousins that were veterans of the Korean War. My family had paid their dues by serving this country. There was a strong sense of pride and a Spirit of Patriotism instilled in all of the family, about being an American.

At this same time, there were two countries shooting satellites into space. The space race was on and the first humans went into space. The Russians put the first human in space and the United States had the Mercury Seven Astronauts. President John Kennedy had been sworn in, and he made the space race into a race to the moon. We learned in school about the assassination of President Lincoln. I was sitting in my high school history class and the only classroom in the school with a television. My teacher turned on the television and we were shocked with the assassination of President Kennedy. We were actually seeing history in the making. Could this really be happening? We watched the horrors of the news broadcast. This time there was television with the whole coverage, along with the passion, sadness and visual scenes. The pictures on the screen were in black and white. The entire event was impressed in our minds.

Race relations had become a big issue in the South. With the television, the incidents were brought into your home. We learned that Rosa Parks, a Black woman had refused to move out of her seat on the bus, for a White person to sit. We would later know her as the Mother of the Civil Rights Movement. Negroes wanted to be called Blacks and were looking for their equal rights. They wanted to vote and to live wherever they wanted to, the same rights that the majority of White Society enjoyed. We watched on television, White policemen beating protesters in Alabama. The White Citizens turned on fire hoses and the unleashing of dogs on the Black Protestors. There were separate water fountains and bathrooms for Whites and Blacks. Certain stores had separate lunch counters for Blacks to eat at, while other stores would not serve them. These people called Americans were battling trying to keep denying other Americans from getting an equal education, an equal opportunity and even voting, just because of the color of their skin. This was segregation at its best and was a disgraceful way of treating America's fellow citizens.

Two Societies living in one country, separate but definitely not equal. This was very true and things had to change. There was a whole social revolution occurring. It was long overdue. I had not experienced any discriminatory actions against me. My relatives in the South knew all about it, but I was living in the North. It really did not make any sense to me. Racial and Social injustices seemed to be in another world far away. It was okay to fight and die for your country. However, you couldn't vote or enjoy the same freedoms as other Americans. My country was hating its own citizens, because of the color of their skin, even if they had been born in this country. I had been taught in school that when you are born in a country, you automatically become a citizen of that country. You are supposed to enjoy the rights and freedoms of that citizenship. This was not true in this country. How do you live in a country with a double standard? What were the added pressures of being Black in this country? This would be a greater learning experience than what was ever being taught in any classroom, in any school.

Blacks had fought and died for this country, as far back as before the Revolutionary War. A Black man was the first person to die in the Boston Massacre. There is a Black man in the boat of the picture of George Washington's Crossing of the Delaware River. Who was he and why was he there? Blacks had served and fought during the American Civil War. They enlisted into the Union Army and also into the Confederate Army. Both sides fought for what they thought was right. The Southern Blacks were protecting the land that they lived on and were not fighting against slavery. On both sides they found themselves as victims of war. President Lincoln had freed the slaves, but nothing had changed. There were Jim Crow Laws that were passed to keep Blacks from getting a good education and an equal opportunity to make a living in this country. A hundred years later and things were still not equal. Black citizens were still being lynched and killed, because they spoke their minds or walked on the wrong side of the street. Those in the Ku Klux Klan were on the move and terrorizing the Black Americans. The Klan was an overt but secret part of society. The vast majority of White America did not care what was happening and just turned their heads to the Klans' actions.

The Armed Services had been segregated before and during World War II. At the beginning of the war, Blacks could be cooks, grave diggers, and supply in the Quartermaster Corps. They could not serve in a combat outfit. They were not even considered to be first class citizens. I learned that during World War II, German prisoners of war were being transported to Kansas or Oklahoma for detention. They were traveling by train through the Southern parts of this country. When the train stopped, the Germans could go into the dining areas and get some food, or use the bathrooms. The Military Police Guards, who were Black, could not go into the same dining areas or use the same bathrooms as the prisoners. The Prisoners of War had more rights and were treated better than their guards. When White Americans saw the German prisoners, it was said, "They look just like us." These were the same people that were killing and fighting their brothers and fathers. They were the enemy in the war. There was no hatred for them, but these feelings weren't the same for their guards.

Despite their mistreatment, the Black Guards did their job. All Americans were not being treated the same, especially by other Americans.

The 1950's and 60's brought about the rise of Rev. Martin Luther King and his nonviolent approach to changing the way things were being done. The Freedom Riders rode buses to the South. White supporters and Blacks sat in places where the White Southerners did not allow this to happen. Violence was used against them. They were arrested and went to jail, over and over again. All of these arrests were for basic human rights. Things were going to be settled in a court of law. At the same time, Malcolm X was calling for an armed rebellion in the Black community to get the Rights that they deserved. There was a call for the Blacks to go back to Africa, by some of the White Majority. The Black Panther Party was formed and they were the militant part of the Black Community. All of this was needed to bring notice to what was going on in this country. There would be no more standing on the sidelines or watching the world go by. The feelings were at the point of getting involved in what was going on. The Federal Government had a job to do.

Now here is a real dilemma, which of these groups should I belong to. I listened to both sides and they had their own points of view. Dad always said, "Don't follow the crowd, be your own man." He also taught us that we could be anything we wanted to be and that we were no better than anyone else. We would have to work harder to get whatever we wanted. He wanted us to shoot for the top of anything we wanted to do and to be the best. If we fell short, we would have made it further than anyone else had gone. He wanted us to do our best. Dad said, "I do not want any of my sons working in the factories." The factories were dirty, greasy and very noisy. This was the time before safety standards, computers and robots. They all worked very hard. He wanted his sons to have a better life than what he had. He also said that he didn't care what we

4

wanted to be. If we wanted to be a bum on the street, then we had better be the best damn bum on the street.

To Mom and Dad education was the only answer. Knowledge is Power. They also taught us never to forget who you were, where you came from and how you got there. You cannot accomplish anything by yourself. You are standing on the shoulders of those that came before you. We owed the past generations to do better in the future. This was hard to understand at such a young age, but it was appreciated in my later years.

I was about to be the first of their sons to graduate from high school and was not going to college. Being the oldest, it seemed like I was paving the way for my brothers, having to experience things in life first. I had to decide what to do and what I thought was right for me. No one was going to tell me what to do or how to act. The choices were to either go to work or the military. It was my decision to make of what I was going to do with my life. I made that decision. This is my country — Right or Wrong.

My parents were not the happiest people in the world, but I had made up my mind. I could have joined the work force as an automobile mechanic, but didn't want that right now. I had to walk my own road and I believed that it was my turn to serve my country. I was joining the military and wanted to join the Marines. Mom said, "Why the Marines, they always go in first?" During the wars, she had read the stories about the exploits of the Marines in the newspapers.

I told Mom, the Marines were the best and that is what I wanted to be. Dad didn't say anything, but you could tell by the expression on his face that he wasn't really happy. Superman has x-ray vision, but Dad had a stare that could cut through steel. With just a glance of his eyes, you knew that you were in trouble and no words were needed. I was hit by the stare as

I began to plead my case. I was almost 18 years old, ready to graduate and take my place in society.

I had learned to repair cars in high school. I wanted to expand my education and repair airplanes. I would now let the government teach me. I knew that there were dangers of joining the military. There was a small war brewing in a little country in Southeast Asia named South Vietnam, half way around the world. This really didn't concern me. I would be working on aircraft and not fighting in a war.

MAKING OF A MARINE

After graduating high school in June, I was bound for the United States Marine Corps. I had enlisted on the delay entry program, along with the aviation-guaranteed program. This gave me the summer to have some fun. These days went by very fast.

In August 1965, I left for Parris Island. The first stop was Hartford, Connecticut and a ride to Springfield, Massachusetts, where I was getting my first airplane ride, courtesy of the United States Government. One of my Kaynor Tech High School classmates was with me. Johnny Baker and I had enlisted on the buddy plan. We were staying together for boot camp. Johnny had been with me in Walsh Grammar School and High School. We were growing up or I should call it maturing or another step toward adulthood?

We arrived at Springfield, Mass. and boarded a two engine, propeller driven DC-3 passenger airplane. We were flying to Beaufort, South Carolina. This was my first airplane ride. I must admit it that I was scared. The sun had set, when we boarded the plane. The engines started with a roar and I watched the fire coming out of the exhaust. We rolled onto the runway and my heart began racing. We began to roll faster and faster, down the runway and we took off. The airplane lifted into the sky. It was like riding in an elevator, as my heart rose in my chest. We slowly went higher and higher as I watched the houses and cars get smaller and smaller, in the ever growing darkness. Somewhere over New Jersey, there was a baseball game being played in a stadium. The people that were watching the game didn't even notice the transport aircraft flying overhead. This plane carried recruits, who were going to learn how to protect their freedoms. Did they even care? It was at night and looked strange, as we were looking down on the world from a different prospective. Out of a sea of blackness were dots of lights, which were cities. The flight was really enjoyable, as well as exciting. After a few hours, we landed at the airport in South Carolina.

We exited the airplane and walked into the terminal and the bathroom. Suddenly, someone yelled, "Get out here!" We all came running out like someone had done something wrong. There stood a Marine. He stood straight and tall and was not smiling. He said for us to get our stuff, go outside and get into the bus. Well, we ran outside, but there was no bus. There was a tractor trailer, but no bus. We were all standing there, looking around for the bus. The Marine yelled and pointed, "Get in that cattle's car!" The trailer was made to carry people, but there were no seats. When we got in, there were benches. We could not even see out of the trailer that had wire mesh near the top, but there were no windows. This was the mode of transportation that took us to the Marine Corps Recruit Depot at Parris Island, S.C., in the dead of night.

We were taken directly to processing. It was about midnight and there was a lot of paperwork that had to be filled out. They ran us from one room to another, with plenty of forms in each one. At about 3:00 a.m., they showed us to a squad bay that was lined with bunk beds. We were told to go to bed and get some sleep. At approx. 5:00 a.m., a Drill Instructor threw a garbage can down the aisle and began to yell for us to get up. The noise was so loud that it made me rise up about two feet off of the bed. He told us to stand at attention in front of the bunks. We were in a complete of state of shock. At this point, I knew that I was in the wrong place and began to think about what I had done. I knew that I wanted to be a Marine and this was boot camp. This was still the middle of the night for me and I should have been sleeping. I was thinking about becoming a Marine when the sun came up. Well, we were running around again for some more processing. It was in one room and then to another. We ran everywhere, there was no walking.

At approx. 7:00 a.m., we were taken to the mess hall for breakfast. We lined up and went through the chow line, doing a side step. There was no talking. We held our trays against our chests. When we reached the server, the tray was held out in front of us and the food was placed on it. The food was carried to the benches and placed on the table. No one could eat until the last person was served. The Drill Instructor told us to sit down by saying, "Ready Seats!" Well, we all had to seat down at the same time. Of course, this did not happen and after several attempts, we finally sat down. There was no talking as we sat looking straight ahead. We were told to sit up straight and to eat a square meal. We were to take the fork, get some food, while looking straight ahead. The fork was then raised to eye level and then brought the food directly to the mouth. This was at a 90-degree angle, a square meal. After taking first bite, we were told to stand up and pick up our trays. We were then shown where the garbage cans were. We then were instructed to empty the entire breakfast into the trash. After dumping our food, we then ran out of the mess hall. This was my first meal in the Marine Corps. Talk about fast food.

After breakfast, the sun was up and they began to issue us the things that we needed: clothes, boots, blanket and linen. We went to the barracks, and this was the First Battalion. The buildings were two-story, wooden style that overlooked the parade field on one end and the swamps on the other end. The next stop was to the barber. Some of the White recruits had long hair. Some of them cried when they received their first haircut. They took shears and cut your hair. Your entire head, every inch of your head, was smooth. When we left, there was no hair on your head at all, not one blade of hair. We were all the same, at least with bald heads.

We were then taken to eat lunch and dinner, but it was the same routine, "Ready Seats" and a square meal and no talking. This time we were able to eat the entire meal. We were assigned a bed on the first floor of the barracks. This would be our home and the people would be our platoon. The platoon was made up of individuals from the northern and southern parts of the country. We made our beds and stored the other gear that had been given to us — all military government issue. At the end of the day, we were told to write a letter home. We were told to tell our parents that we had arrived safely and that we were having a wonderful time. We packed up our civilian clothes and sent them home.

The Drill Instructor (D. I.) came in and walked up and down the middle of the barracks. He was shouting about what he wanted done every day. He said, "I am your mother, father, priest, and everyone else but I am not your Friend." He then opened the back door to the barracks and pointed at the swamps. It was just like the movie "The D. I." starring Jack Webb. There were the swamps and then the ocean. He said that there were snakes in the swamps and sharks in the ocean before you could get to the land on the other side. He said that there are two ways to get off of the island. You could go this way, while pointing to the ocean or you can graduate and ride out the main gate on graduation day. If you do decide to leave during the night, leave a note on your pillow so you could be accounted for. He said several recruits had attempted this escape, but no one had ever made it. Some had died trying. How bad could the training be? I knew that they could not do enough to make me try to go through the swamps.

Now it started getting rough. We ran everywhere, physical training was critical. The temperature was in the 90's and it was humid. We would start before the sun came up. P.T. (Physical Training) was the first thing that was done each and every morning. It was exercises and running. We would come back and take a shower, all before breakfast. Then there were classes on military life, edict, history and more P.T. and more. The idea of this boot camp was to break everyone down mentally and physically, then rebuild you into a Marine. It was the way that everyone started out the same. No one was any better than anyone else, a chain is as strong as its weakest link and many more sayings were drilled into our heads day after day. They called us every name in the book, but a child of God or a Marine. This is what it took to make a Marine. You start from the bottom and build a new man. We were getting stronger. Was it degrading? Absolutely! If it wasn't like that then I would have been disappointed. Well, I definitely was not disappointed.

The training came hot and heavy. I learned there was only one thing that could stop me and it was me-myself. I learned confidence not only in myself, but also in my fellow recruits. The Drill Instructor told Johnny Baker to get down and start doing pushups and told the rest of us to keep up with him. Well, I knew Johnny from both grammar school and high school. He never lifted any weighs, he just did pushups. He had a strong body and it was chiseled, with muscles popping out all over. Needless to say, he ran us all into the ground. When it was too hot to drill on the parade deck, we did the P. T. in the barracks and there was no air conditioning. It was above 90 outside, and no telling what it was on the inside. The sweat ran like water, but we got stronger and harder.

Swimming was not my strong point. They divided us up into two groups, floaters and non floaters. I was definitely a non floater. I had the buoyancy of a rock. If you wanted to know what was on the bottom of the water, just throw me in. I could walk out. So they taught us to do a travel stroke. We had to swim six widths of the pool. Well I jumped into the water. The depth was about eight feet deep. I began swimming doing this stroke. I made three and a half widths and began to sink, feet first. I struggled to get back to the surface, to no avail. Someone jumped into the water and pulled me out. I drank some water, but I was okay. The Drill Instructor came over to me and asked me if I was all right and I replied, "Yes Sir." He said, "Well you are going back into the water again." I jumped back into the water and began swimming the widths of the pool again. This time I made it three and half times and sank again. I was pulled out again. I was standing on the side of the pool with the others that did not qualify as a swimmer. I had swum seven widths, while those that qualified only had to swim six. The Drill Instructor came down the line and asked each recruit why he did not qualify. Each one gave their excuse and promptly got their punishment. When he got to me, I told him that I was pulled out of the pool twice. It made me proud when he said this one would not quit. I still couldn't swim, but I did not quit.

Being raised in the North, this was my first real encounter with White Southerners. After watching the Civil Right Marchers in Alabama, with the fire hoses and police dogs, I really did not know what to expect. I learned that we were all recruits and it did not matter what color you were or where you came from. We all were green and we would all be MARINES, if you graduated. If you haven't been through it then you wouldn't understand it. It was off to the rifle range and we learned to shoot. Your rifle is your best friend. A Marine is a rifleman first. The most dangerous person on the planet is a Marine who has just graduated from Boot Camp.

Along came the final tests, which included a march to a place called Elliot's Beach. There was a five-mile march at the end of it. There went my luck again, and I had a cold. We were marching then we were running and then marching again. My nose was running and my eyes were watering. I couldn't see where I was going. My Squad Leader was White and from Alabama. He told me to slip my hand through his blanket roll strap on his back pack. He would guide me through the run. The recruit on the side of me wanted to take my rifle for me. I wouldn't let him. A Marine never gives up his weapon. I completed the run. Imagine a guy from the Deep South leading me through the run. Maybe they all weren't as bad or like what I had seen on television. I was learning about people and having faith in my fellow recruits. We had become a team and a fighting force.

Graduation day came, which was one of the proudest days of my life. I had earned the right to be called MARINE. On this day, our Drill Instructors referred to us as MARINES. We had joined the family, America's Fighting Force. We had completed the training and we were actually Marines. Relatives and friends were allowed on the base. After the parade and ceremonies, we packed our gear and headed for the buses. This time, they were real buses and not the cattle cars. Sergeant Cleveland came onto the bus and said, "Private Armstrong, you still owe me twenty." Private Armstrong got down in the aisle of the bus and started doing pushups. When he reached ten, the D. I. stopped him and said he could pay him the others when he came back through boot camp. The respect for them is never lost. Thank you to our Drill Instructors for what they had accomplished. You never forget your Drill Instructors. They were S/Sgt. Albright, Sgt. Ciampa and Sgt. Cleveland. They would be ready for the next batch of recruits. As for us, they had taken a bunch of raw civilians and had transformed us. We were now brand new Marines.

The buses took us out of the main gate and up the highway to Camp Geiger in North Carolina. This trip was for our Infantry Training Regiment (ITR) instruction. This was where we got to develop our infantry skills. We fired all types of weapons, learned combat tactics and developed more confidence in the other Marines. We all had a new found sense of pride in ourselves. Actually we didn't need a bus; we could have flowed all the way to the new base. After a month, I left there for Memphis, Tennessee and my Aviation Schools. I didn't see Johnny Baker again for the rest of our tour of duty. He went in a different direction for his military occupational specialty training.

SEMPER FIDELIS
means
ALWAYS FAITHFUL

TIME FOR SCHOOL

The military took me to Raleigh, North Carolina and flew me by a four-engine propeller-driven passenger airplane to Atlanta, Georgia. From there it was by a Boeing 707 jet airliner to Memphis, Tennessee. Now this was traveling in style, four jet engines! This airplane was quieter compared to the other planes that I had flown down here in and it was fast. We landed in Memphis in no time. This was almost half of the way across the country. We were taken by bus to a small town called Middleton, where the aviation schools were located on the Naval Base.

I was getting so far away from the safety of home. There was some nervousness about being on my own for the first time. I settled into the living quarters in the barracks. Things were okay, except for my pay being screwed up. It was now November 1965 and no pay. I had to start borrowing money at crazy interest rates, but you have to live on something. Food and Housing were provided, but not anything extra. I had to learn to survive. My schools were not scheduled to start yet. I called my mother and told her that I wanted to come home for Christmas, but I did not have any money. She sent me $50.00. It was sweet of her but that was not even a drop in the bucket. After paying back the money that I owed, I was left with almost nothing.

So what does a good son do? I called Mom back and told her the situation that I was in. She then sent me $150.00 and told me to come home the fastest way possible. I went to the reservation counter and learned that all of the flights out of Memphis were booked. I then went to the bus station and learned the same thing. Everyone was going home for the holidays. Well that only left the train. It was called the Orange Blossom Special going to Washington, D.C. So I left Memphis, with another Marine who was going to Baltimore and a Sailor. We had a quart of rum with us and it was off we go, heading home for the holidays. This train was the slowest mode of travel and it was supposed to be an express. Well it stopped for every train going in the opposite direction. The train actually stopped, someone got off, ran across a field, handed a lady a package and then jumped back onto the train. The rum did make the ride a little more pleasant.

Upon arriving in Washington, we went our separate ways. I never saw those two again, but we had a good time on the train. I then took a cab to the airport and caught a flight to New York. After landing, I then took a bus from the airport to the Port Authority, in New York. There I took a bus to Waterbury and finally took a cab to my house. When I walked into the house, Mom said, "What took you so long to get home?" I told her that I had taken every mode of transportation to get there. It took 32 hours. They all were glad to see me. This was the first time any one of her children had been gone from home for more than a week. I was tired, but I was glad to be home.

I sat down at the kitchen table, took out a cigarette and lit it. She said, "Oh, you are now smoking?" She didn't know it but I was smoking in high school. Then again maybe she did know it, but I never got caught. Now for my brother, Greg had been caught smoking before. Dad walked in and naturally there was no emotion. He said sarcastically, "Well a big time Marine" and I replied with pride, "that's right." I could see a lot of pride in him, but he never said anything. He took me down to his favorite bar, the Cherry Restaurant, also known as the Cherry Rest or the White Front, where all of his friends were at. They were the ones that he grew up with and he had served with during World War II. I think that he was showing me off, but I was young and really didn't realize it. I was only 18 and the legal drinking age was 21, so all that I could have was soda. It felt really good to be standing at the bar, with my father. I wasn't that high school kid anymore, which was only four months earlier. It was a totally different experience, being respected as a Marine. I could fight and die for this country, but couldn't vote or have a drink.

While I was at home, I just had to try my luck. Dad was always so big. He stood 6' 4" tall and about 230 pounds. He said to me that I thought that I was something. I replied to him kiddingly, "You can't do twenty pushups." He dropped to the kitchen floor and pushed out twenty. This shocked me. Mom couldn't believe her eyes, either. He got up and just gave me one of those looks like, "You don't beat your father." Nothing more had to be said. He was still the best, even though I could have done a lot more. Dad was 41 years old and I was a lot younger.

I found my girlfriend, Mary Alice. She was a sight for sore eyes. We went out and tried to catch up with the missing months. I went back to my high school to see Mr. James White, my History Teacher and a former Marine. There was a gleam in his eyes when he saw me. I saw my other teachers and students that I knew. Something had changed, but at that time I really couldn't see exactly what. Later I learned that it was me that had changed. The safety of my school and friends was gone. I was now on my own and growing up.

The smell of Mom's cooking really brought the holidays to life. There were the Christmas tree and presents, but there was nothing like being around the family after the months of training and schools. I really felt good. We sang Christmas Carols. Everyone has to speak of why we were thankful and that we were being together as a family. The family rituals seemed to have more of an impact on me. After Christmas, it was time for me to return to Memphis. Mary Alice took a picture of all of us, which turned out to be the only family picture that we would ever have taken. I jumped on the bus for the 18-hour ride back to Memphis. It was faster than taking the train.

Front Row: Milton Jr., Mom, Reggie
Back Row: Milton Sr., Greg, Sam

I must admit that I was "squared away" (meaning looking good or sharp). I had gone into the service weighing about 150 lbs. I was now weighing 170 lbs. and was looking good in my uniform. Our classes started right away. I was walking down the street on the base and noticed some Marines doing some twirling of their rifles and they were sharp. I asked them who they were and the Marines said that they were the Drill Team. I asked him, "How do you join?" One of the Marines said to me that I couldn't make it. He handed me his rifle and I began to perform a few tricks that I had learned in the Young Marines. After he saw what I could do, he brought me to Corporal Jiminez, who was in charge of the unit. I became a member of the Drill Team. I wanted to be a part of the best.

The Drill Team and its practices added more work to my schedule. It was classes all day and then two to three hours of practice and then there was the studying. We were drilling with M-1 rifles with 16" chrome bayonets. We starched our uniforms very tight and spit shined our boots so they looked like glass mirrors. We knew that we were the best on the base. It was February 1966, when I got my Dress Blue Uniform. Now, I not only felt like a Marine, but looked like a Marine.

The first school was for mechanical fundamentals. It was really boring to me. They broke everything down to a level so that the slowest person could understand it. It started off with this is a wrench and this is a nut, it turns to the right to tighten and to the left to loosen. This is a screwdriver and the different types of screws. Well after four years in Kaynor Tech and graduating as an automobile mechanic, this seemed silly, but I had to complete this school. I was very bored and was constantly falling asleep in the class. It was so bad that the instructor took me into the hallway and handed me a propeller blade. I had to do the manual of arms with it. He told me that if I flunked his class, I was going to be shipped to the infantry as a 0311, rifleman and I would be a Grunt. After a couple of weeks, I took the test and passed it with a grade of 93. The instructor said that I could sleep in all of his classes, if I could keep getting those kind of marks.

After that, there was no more sleeping in class, now we were learning about aircraft engines and their maintenance. Now they had my attention. After working on six cylinder and V-8 engines in high school, now it was 1820 radial aircraft engines. As a mechanic, I was in my glory. I just knew that I would be working on some big transport aircraft and flying all over the world. Well, I was wrong and it was not to be. The next school was helicopter repair. It was on to helicopter systems; hydraulics, rotors, and powerplants. By rights, a helicopter is not supposed to be able to fly, but it does. It is like a bumblebee, whose body is bigger than its wings. It had a lot of moving parts that all had to work together. There was a lot to learn. The helicopter is a very complex machine and I had to learn it all.

To be a member of an aircrew, you have to be at least a second class swimmer. I was a non-qualified swimmer. It was back to the swimming pool again. I was a weak swimmer, but I had to do it their way and that didn't work. They took us up the tower and strapped me into a parachute harness. This was to simulate entering the water with a parachute. They swung me out over the water, about 15 feet in the air. Now if the Instructor liked you, he would release you so that you went straight into the water. If he didn't like you, he would release you either when your back or face was facing the water. This resulted in a belly flop or you landed on your back, in the water. Well my Instructor didn't like me, but seeing that I was a non-qualified swimmer, he had to drop me right. I was swinging and he released me. I went right into the water. I hit the bottom and pushed up to the surface. There were two divers in the pool, for safety. One of them asked me if I was okay and I replied sure and swam to the side of the pool and got out. The instructor thought that I was playing around. I told him that I was a weak swimmer, with the buoyancy of a rock. He thought that I was trying to get over on him.

The next stop was to the big pool. I was told that I had to swim the length of the pool, back and forth to qualify as a second class swimmer. He said that I could do any stroke that I thought that I could do. I got into the pool and did the backstroke. I went all the way down and came back. I got tired. I found a small ledge on the side of the pool and I began pushing off of it. I grabbed the ladder along the side of the pool and pushed off of it. With all of this I became a second class swimmer. It was just another adventure in getting what I wanted.

The Drill Team was going to Corpus Christi, Texas for an exhibition. We flew on a DC-3. While part of the team slept, I was wide awake. I was listening to the engines, but they just didn't sound right to me. I guess that it was just the mechanic in me. We arrived safely and got ready for our demonstration. We marched into a football stadium that had more than 100,000 people and we were a part of the parade. I had never seen so many people. The announcer called us the Marine Corps Silent Drill Team from Memphis. Well we weren't silent, but Cpl. Jiminez gave the commands softly as we performed our maneuvers and rifle drill around the track of the stadium.

The next stop was a special demonstration. Seeing that the team had taken first place the year before, we were not in competition this year. It was a good thing, because everything started going wrong. We marched into the gym of a school. As we were performing, one of the bayonets let go and it flew over the entire platoon, hit the floor and slid across the floor. The next thing, it was my turn. I twirled my rifle, when the entire barrel and receiver came loose, and struck me in the head as it fell to the floor. I was left with the wooden stock in my hands. The funny thing was that I never knew that anything was wrong and I kept on doing the drill. One of the other guys said port arms, port arms. I finally went to port arms and we marched off of the floor. An Officer had seen what had happened and he came up to me. He said that was the finest recovery that he had ever seen. I told him that I didn't even know anything was wrong. We both smiled.

I was glad to return to Memphis. Thee team performed in a stadium in Memphis. We were on line and doing a drill called "The Kiss Of Death". One of the guys began the drill and the bayonet cut the front of his Dress Blues. This didn't stop the performance. I often wondered if these things ever happened to the Marine Corps Silent Drill Team at Eighth and I, in Washington. They were the best. I know that it does, but the crowd will never see it.

We did get weekend liberty. This meant that we could go to Memphis for some partying. This was my first trip away from home and being let loose on a town. They told us that Beale Street was out of bounds, off limits and that we could not go there. Well, you know what that means. We made a natural beeline there. This was the Black section of the town, and the home of Jazz music. It was dirty and we watched each other's back, even when we got drunk. There still was a lot of fear about being out on my own, I guess that I never really got over that feeling. I was a Marine now and nothing was too scary for me. One weekend, there was a Klu Klux Klan rally being held in downtown Memphis. I was told not to go into Memphis. You didn't have to tell me twice and for that weekend I stayed on the base. We developed our own saying named for the K. K. K., and it was the Kool Kolored Kids. We had our own music and believe me, we stayed away from the Klan. This was America and I didn't like it. I was learning about the South.

I met some very nice people in Memphis. I am trying to remember how I met Peggy. She was a little heavy but she was nice. She brought me home to her family and they all liked me. I now had some place to go when I came to town. She had two sisters that were knockouts. I had my friend Kermit McNair with me and introduced him to them. He really liked Charlene. We partyed the rest of the time while we were stationed there. There was also Defrances. I really liked her. She was in the Navy. I know how I met her, and it was at the U. S. O.. We danced and partyed together. She was later transferred to a base in Texas. After leaving Memphis, I never saw her again. It seemed like nothing was permanent. Friendships were made and then we went in different directions. You're here today and gone tomorrow. I thought that maybe this is what military life was supposed to be.

May 1966, came graduation day and we received our assignments. I was going to the New River Air Station in Jacksonville, North Carolina. I was now a helicopter mechanic and ready for my first duty station. First of all, there was some leave coming and another long bus ride across the country to home. The bus headed north as I thought about what I had accomplished over the past months. I had completed boot camp and my aviation schools. Now, I could work on helicopters.

I arrived home on a Thursday and went to see Mary Alice. She was a senior and still in high school, so I had to wait for her to get out. We spent the rest of the day together. I got around to see some of my other friends. Mary's mother did like me as much as any mother could love a man trying to screw her daughter. There was Friday and Saturday and we were always together. It was boyfriend and girlfriend at its best. On Sunday we went to church in the morning and then went to our separate homes for dinner. I then borrowed Dad's car and picked Mary Alice up. While we were riding, she said that Tony and Greg were going into the Marines, the following week. I had not seen them since I had become a Marine. I had grown up with them and they were good friends. We had been members of the Young Marine Program. Tony had been in the same platoon with me. This platoon was known as the Recons and we were the drill team. They would be leaving for boot camp and it would be a while before I would be seeing them again. I thought that I could give them some insight into what they were heading into. I made an U-turn and went and picked them up. I then drove Mary Alice home.

I dropped Mary Alice off at her house. I told her that we three were going to the drive in. She got out of the car and went into the house. Tony, Greg and I went to my house and told my father where we were going. Mom said that Mary Alice had called a couple of times. The phone then rang and it was her. She was mad that I had dropped her off and did not take her along. I told her that I would see her the next day. She was not satisfied with this. She began yelling at me that I was treating her like Leon (her former boyfriend). At this point I told her, she could go back to Leon, if she wanted to and I hung up the phone. The three of us went to the drive in and had some guy fun. The weekend was over and it was time to get to work at my military job.

On Tuesday, I left for New River, without saying another word or even a goodbye to Mary Alice. How things can change so suddenly from happiness to the sadness of breaking up. Cold, I guess so. I was not having anything to do with petty childhood spats. Life was changing and so was I. It would be a long bus ride down the east coast of the country to my new base. My training was over and I was looking forward to working at my first duty station.

REALITY CHECK

I was assigned to Marine Air Group 26 (MAG 26) and working at H & MS - 26 (HAMS), which was a Headquarters and Maintenance Squadron. This squadron didn't do any flying, just the maintenance that couldn't be done on the operational squadron level. Upon reporting in and finding my living space in the barracks, I went to work in the repair shop. I was working on carburetors and throttle boxes for the CH-34 Helicopters. This was June 1966 and it was all good. I was getting paid. The base was nice, but without a car, I was limited in where I could go. There was always the bus into town or you could hitch a ride there. Life was good. It was like working a regular 8 to 4 job. Of course, there were the duty weekends, but this comes with the job. I was working as a mechanic and still learning my job.

It was in July of 1966, when I received the news one of my friends had been killed in Vietnam. This was Norman Dawson, of whom we called Junior. He had enlisted in the Marine Corps in January 1965. We had been members of the Young Marine Program in Waterbury and he was in my Recon Drill Team Platoon. Tony and Greg were also friends of Junior. They were in boot camp and could not come home for the funeral. Junior did not complete High School, but joined the Marines. I don't think that I ever saw him again after he enlisted and had his leave. He was a Marine only a little more than a year. He was a Grunt, meaning his job was the infantry — 0311 a rifleman was his Military Occupational Specialty. Junior was dead and there was a deep sinking feeling that came over me. This was a big shock and a fact of life had come home to me. Before this, it was always training, building confidence, learning Marine history, making you into a man, and a Marine. We believed that we could walk on water. Now the truth comes out, "You could get killed doing this job". We were mortal.

I went to the maintenance office and requested leave to attend Norman's funeral. The leave was granted. When I went back to pick up my leave papers, I was handed checkout papers. I was being transferred to HMM-262 (Helicopter Marine Medium - 262), an operational squadron that was using the CH-46A, a jet helicopter. There were many Marines on the base that were volunteering to join this squadron, but not me. I was a reciprocating (piston driven) engine mechanic and knew nothing about these jet engines. I was told the Corps would take care of that. The worst kept secret on the base was that in December this entire squadron was going to be deployed to South Vietnam. Well, here I was going to this squadron. How was I going to tell my mother? What was she going to think? I was going to Vietnam. I would be going to war.

Bingo ----- Reality Check ----- The Marine Corps!!

I boarded a bus and settled into my seat for the long ride to Waterbury. The tires of the bus made a soothing hum that helped me to relax. There was too much time for thinking. What had happened to Junior? How did he die? All the way home, I was wondering what I was going to say to Mom. How was I going to tell her that I was going to Vietnam? I pondered this question over and over in my mind, but there was no answer. I got home and walked in the door. Mom started right in on me. She said, "See what happens when you go to Vietnam, Junior is Dead! I don't want you going over there." I listened for a while, mainly because I couldn't get a word in edge wide. When she gets on a roll, there was no stopping her. She went up one side of me and down the other, like only a mother can do. Finally, I blew up. I told her that I did not have to volunteer for Vietnam. They are sending me there! Mom became very quiet, and looked like she was in a state of shock. She listened to me and what I had to say. I showed her the checkout papers and told her the story. She said, "Those papers don't mean anything. You're not going to Vietnam!" Mom had spoken and there was nothing else to be said.

The next day, I went to see Mrs. Dawson and her family. She had told me not to wear my uniform. I walked to her house and up the driveway. There were people standing on the front porch. I walked into the house, as I had done so many times before. Mrs. Dawson looked at me and began to cry. I reminded her too much of Junior. We were about the same size and age and we had been friends growing up. She told me her son, Ricky was escorting Junior's body home from California. Ricky was in the Air Force. I later met with the local Marine Recruiter and the Chaplain. They said I was going to be the Official Escort for Junior, when his body arrived home. This was an enormous honor for me. I was a Private First Class, been in the Marines for almost a year, and here I was going to be an Official Escort. The next question was, what was an escort? I had to be told what the duties entailed. I was going to be the Official Representative for the Marine Corps to Junior's family.

I was told how Junior had died. He had been shot several times by an enemy machine gun during an operation in Vietnam. I was not to tell the family about this at this time. It is one thing to be an Official Representative and not knowing the people that are involved and another thing to be personally involved. Although, you understand and feel for the people and what they are going through, you are not emotional attached to them. Junior and I had gone to school, played and had grown up together. We had eaten at each other's homes. We knew each other's families. Now Junior's life was over. I was deeply emotionally involved. I was like a member of his family. I didn't know it then, but this would be one of the hardest assignments I could ever have.

Mrs. Dawson told me of what she had done when the Military Representatives came to her door, with the news about Junior. She said that she really wasn't very nice to them. But then again, what would you expect? You know why they have come, but you don't want to hear what they have to say. I told her that they understood. She was holding a picture of Junior, as she sat in the chair. It was his graduation picture from boot camp. She said, he was so proud to be a Marine. I stayed for a while and then told her that I would be at my house and if she needed anything, for her to call me. I would take care of it. This was my job and I would do anything for Junior and his family and now it was official. I went home and got my Dress Blues Uniform ready. My mother still wasn't happy. My father didn't say anything. I think that I would have been shocked, if he had said to me what his feelings were. Norman was one of the first persons from Waterbury that had been killed in Vietnam and the first Marine. He would not be the last, before the war was over.

Norman's body was delivered to the Pentecostal Assembly Church on Cherry Street. The red brick church was at the bottom of the hill, where I lived and it was surrounded by one of the many factories in town. The wake was scheduled from 2 to 4 P.M. and 7 to 9 P.M. It was about 1:30 P.M., when Mrs. Dawson and I arrived and walked into the church. The church was very warm, but we really didn't notice it. We were alone. The church was empty and dark, as we entered through the front doors. There were soft lights at the end of the center aisle. They were shining on the casket in front of the altar. We began to walk arm in arm, down the aisle. It seemed like a mile long, as we slowly approached the casket. About halfway down the aisle, Mother D, as we called her, began to tremble and squeezing my arm. She began sobbing and saying, Oh No! She called his name, over and over. She called to Junior, but he could not hear her. I held her up as we got closer to the body of her son, my friend, my fellow Marine.

The casket was open and half covered with an American Flag. Junior was dressed in his Dress Blues and he looked like he was asleep. There was no waking him up. We stood there for several minutes, as she cried and touched his face softly. We then sat down, while the rest of the family came into the church. One by one, they approached the casket and viewed Junior lying there, motionless. They began to cry and helped each other to walk slowly to their seats in the pews.

The tears flowed like a river throughout the entire wake. Mother D was in a state of shock. No parent wants to lose a child at any age. How do you say goodbye to a piece of you, that you gave birth to and had raised? I must admit that I don't remember much about that day either. Junior's sisters were taking his death very hard. There were hundreds and hundreds of people that had come to pay their respects. Every mother that came was feeling the same hurt and the pain that Mother D and her family were feeling, the loss of a son in war. No one ever wants to sit on the front row of the church at a wake, this means that you are with the immediate family of the deceased. This was the first time I had ever sat there. I sat beside Mother D. and we got through the two hours of receiving mourners and sympathizers. I know that my family had come, but I don't remember them being there.

We left and it was back to the Dawson home. There the family tried to rest and compose themselves. We had to go back to the church from 7 to 9 for the second part of the wake. It was the same thing all over again, hundreds of people. We later returned to the Dawson's home and I stayed there for several hours. A lot of childhood and school friends were there. There was a lot of time reminiscing about our growing up together. I did not tell anyone that I was heading to Vietnam. This was not the time or place. This had been a very long and emotional day. It was not an easy time for any of us.

The next day was the funeral, which was really a blur. I walked to the Dawson home in the morning. This time, I was in my full Dress Blue Uniform. I had warned Mother D that I would have to wear it. She really didn't like it, but there was no way around it. I walked up the long driveway to her house. I entered the house and hugged her. Mother D and I got into the long black limousine, along with the rest of the family for the short ride to the church. What was said and the people that were there, I don't have the slightest idea. I was thinking about what was about to occur, the funeral. The family was in a state of shock. Could this really be happening? There were so many people standing on the sidewalk, as the family cars arrived. The church was filled with people. It was a hot July day and there was no air conditioning in the church. We led the family up the stairs and into the church. We took our seats and the funeral service began. What was said during the service is a complete blank to me. The casket was covered by the American Flag and contained the body of my friend. He was rolled slowly down the aisle at the end of the service and out of the church, as we followed him.

We rode from the church in a long procession to the cemetery in Derby, Connecticut, about twenty miles away. I didn't know why at that time, since he was in Waterbury all of his life. I later learned that he had been born in Derby and that was where Mother D wanted him buried. We rode down the highway and it all was quiet in the limo. Were we really lying Junior to rest? It all seemed like a bad dream, a real nightmare. We arrived at the cemetery and the services were conducted. The Marine Corps did us all proudly; the other Marines, firing squad and bugler. The American Flag was folded and presented to Mother D by a Marine Corps Officer. We stayed at the gravesite for a while, as family and friends kissed Mother D. She left a flower on the casket of her son, before returning to the limo.

As we were riding back to Waterbury, Mother D looked at me and said, "Marines Do Cry." With tears rolling down my cheeks, I replied, "Yes we do." I had maintained a formal, but courteous military attitude, remaining strong for the family throughout the entire ordeal. The hurt and pain of this loss was there, but I could not show it. I had seen everyone's emotions and tears flow throughout the entire time, but I couldn't. I was representing the Marine Corps. I had stood proud, straight and tall. I did my duty for my fellow Marine and his family, now Junior was buried and at rest. I was finally able to release my emotions. Mother D held me as if she was my own mother. This was a very hard day for all of us. My being so close to the family made it was one of the saddest days of my life. To bury a Marine, and a life long childhood friend isn't easy at any age. Junior and I were so very young and his life was now over.

I spent the next couple of days at home and with the Dawson Family, before heading back to North Carolina. Mother D wanted me to write her. I said that I would. I never thought my family might have been thinking that they might have to go through this same thing, if something had happened to me. I was leaving, Mom said that she was praying that I did not have to go to Vietnam. Dad was working, when I left. I again took that bus ride back to the base, with its long hours of riding and lots of time for thinking.

Growing up, we had the idea that kids live forever. Only old people died. Life was nothing but fun and games. We were not poor, but we were all the same, so nobody knew the difference. Our parents worked and the children played together. We had our fun, dances, and girlfriends. Junior had loved the Marine Corps and was proud of what he was doing. It cost him his life. Junior would never grow old. My childhood was really over and the reality of this part of my life was hitting me. I was an adult with adult responsibilities, even though 21 years old was considered to be an adult and I was only 18 years old. I was entering another phase of my life. These memories would stay with me for the rest of my life. The entire ordeal had taken a big emotional toll on me.

OPERATIONAL HELICOPTER SQUADRON - HMM-262

After getting back to the base at New River, I checked into HMM-262. I walked onto the big white concrete flight line. There they were, the big green helicopters parked and shining in the morning sun light. Boeing Aircraft Vertol Division had built the CH-46A model (CH stands for Cargo Helicopter). I looked inside of one of them. It was clean with canvas red seats, gray flooring, and off white insolation along the walls. I looked into the cockpit with all of its gauges. It had the smell of a new car. These were beautiful machines, but they were powered by jet engines. I did not know anything about them. Well, the Marine Corps would take care of that.

I was back in school again. This time I was learning about jet engines and related systems. It was classes on rotors and related systems and everything else about the chopper. There were plenty of inspections to be performed. At the end of two weeks, I was now a jet helicopter mechanic. This helicopter was like a sports car; it had speed and a lifting ability unmatched at the time. It was also a lot quieter than the piston pounding CH-34 that sounded like a car without a muffler. I spent the rest of the month working as a mechanic, refining my skills. I was also learning that the rumors were true. This squadron was going to Vietnam in December.

I was contacted and requested to attend an awards ceremony in Hartford, Connecticut. Mother D was going to receive Norman's Purple Heart, along with his other medals. I came back home again. I joined his family and went to Hartford. We were led into a large conference room where we were seated. Everyone was silent as we sat around the long table. I guess that we all were thinking about Norman and the funeral that had just taken place a few weeks earlier. It all was still fresh in our minds. Why was I here and why was I requested? These questions went through my mind, but I never asked them. His family wanted me there and it was all that mattered.

The room was very quiet with a very somber mood. There was one single fly buzzing around the room, annoying everyone and disrupting the silence. Each person would swat the fly away. It would only fly around to pester another person. The fly came near me and I waved it away. It made a stop at just about everyone in the room. Well, it came back around me again. In an instant, I reached up and grabbed the fly out of the air in my hand. I shook it in my fist, threw the fly to the floor and stepped on it. I never said a word or changed my solemn expression. The entire room broke out in laughter. One person said, "That's what happens when you mess with a Marine". I only smiled. Another Marine entered the room and asked us to follow him.

The entire family filed out of this room and into a large auditorium. There were several other families were gathered on the floor. They had also lost sons in Vietnam. Mother D and I took our position on the floor, along with the other families. The Marine Officers presented themselves to each family and gave to them the medals that their sons were awarded. Then it was our turn. I was the only active duty person there representing a family. I was still a Private First Class. I saluted the Officers and they gave Mother D Norman's medals. I later received a picture that appeared in the newspaper. It showed Mother D and me in the ceremony. I felt deeply honored to be representing Norman's family.

After the ceremony was over, we returned to Waterbury. I went back to my parents' house. I told them I had decided that I didn't just want to repair airplanes and helicopters, but I wanted to fly. This didn't set well with either of them. Neither of them had ever flown in an airplane. I was the first in the family to do that. I really like the feeling of being off of the ground. After a little discussion, which was all negative, I was going to do what I wanted to do.

I returned to the base and learned what it took to be a Crew Chief. A Crew Chief is the person that is in charge of a helicopter, on other aircraft it was the Plane Captain or Flight Engineer. The Crew Chief is a part of the flight crew, which consists of four people. There are two pilots, Command Pilot and Co-pilot, the Crew Chief and Gunner. The crew functions as a team. They have to depend and rely on each other to accomplish the mission, which is to support the troops.

The Crew Chief is the person that insures the flight status and flight safety of the helicopter (MECHANICAL OPERATION), the in-flight mechanic, the right side machine gunner, in charge of the cabin area of the chopper and the load/cargo master. No matter what the rank of the passenger was, the Crew Chief would be in charge and responsible for them, while they were onboard. Emergency procedures had to become a second nature. Every possible system failure had to be known, and what the response was to deal with the problem. There was a great deal to learn and a lot of responsibility. This was the job for me, I wanted to fly and here was my opportunity.

The squadron had 24 helicopters and was made up of 250 Marines, Officers and Enlisted Personnel and very few that were Black. There were no Black Officers, along with only three Black Crew Chiefs and two were Hispanics out of 30 in the outfit. There were several others in the aviation related shops and transportation divisions. There was certain camaraderie between the minorities, but nothing was ever said. It was like we had something to prove. We were there because of our ability to do the job at hand, then again, so were the Tuskegee Airmen of World War Two, who were Black Aviators. The entire ground crew, their mechanics and support personnel were also Black and they had to be special too.

During the month, we had to qualify with the Mae West Life Preserver. We put on the life jacket and headed for a chopper. This was going to be my first flight in a helicopter. About six of us got in and we took off. There was a feeling of excitement as the chopper lifting us up into the air, almost effortlessly. Well, this flight lasted all of what seemed like two minutes. The chopper headed for New River. It circled and landed right in the river. The crewchief lowered the cabin door and said

- everybody out. We quickly moved to the door and jumped into the river. We were supposed to inflate the life jacket and swim over to a raft and the chopper would come back and pick us up. My swimming had not improved and I still had the buoyancy of a rock. I hit the water and immediately began to sink. I popped one of the CO_2 cartridges, which inflated one chamber of the vest. I was still sinking. I popped the other cartridge, inflating another chamber. I popped to the surface, like a cork. I then blew up the third chamber with the air tube. I figured why should I take any chances? It is better to inflate the entire vest and not need it, than to need it and not to have it inflated. I began trying to swim toward the raft, but I was caught in an undertow that was pulling me away from it. The harder I swam, the further I was from the raft. I then heard the sound of the chopper. I looked up and saw that it was landing back in the river. It was closer to me than the raft, so I swam to the chopper and got in. We picked up the others and flew back to the base. These flights continued until the entire squadron was familiarized and qualified in the use of Mae West.

The flight crews trained in choppers for day and night operations. We practiced with fully loaded helicopters, as well as carrying external loads. We could carry 20 combat equipped Marines or 15 stretchers for the wounded. We practiced rescue operations with the cable hoist and harness. The pilots practiced autorotation landings, without power. I learned that the weight and balance of the cargo in the chopper was critical to the flight operation of the chopper. I studied first aid and the emergency procedures, including water landings. I took the written, oral and in-flight tests and passed them all. I was 19 years old now, a qualified Crew Chief and could be responsible for a million-dollar helicopter. I could be a member of a flight crew and I took this awesome responsibility very personally. I was promoted to the rank of Lance Corporal.

The helicopters were fitted with armor plates around the engines and armor plated seats for the pilots. This was the only protection that the chopper had. Large dust filters were installed to protect the engines from the dust and sand of Vietnam. The outside skin of the helicopter is only 30 thousandth of an inch aluminum sheet metal. You could put your hand through it in the right places. A screwdriver could punch a hole in it very easily, not to mention what a bullet could do to it. The chopper is delicate and fragile, but durable.

The next flights were to become qualified as port side aerial gunners with the M-60 machine gun. We learned to hit targets on the ground from a moving chopper. Now, I was a qualified aerial gunner, but did not have a helicopter of my own. We were ready for combat and there was an air of excitement developing in the entire squadron. Everything happened so fast.

November 1966, we had preserved our helicopters to protect them from the salty sea air of its ocean cruise and flew them to Norfolk, Virginia. There they were placed aboard a ship, along with several members of the squadron. They were going to escort the choppers to Vietnam, which was going to take about a month. Talk about a slow boat to China. The rest of us were allowed to go home for a twenty-day leave. We jumped on buses and headed to hundreds of different homes in different states. The trip was going to be different, yet the same for each Marine. Get your life in order, before heading overseas.

I had written Mother D several letters, but I had to stop. From the tone of her letters, I was getting the feeling that she was trying to replace Junior with me. I could not let this happen. I was not helping her by continuing to write. I didn't want her to be receiving any more letters from Vietnam. Upon getting home, I told Mother D that I didn't think that it would be good for her. I would not be writing her from Vietnam, but I would keep in touch.

Upon getting home, I told Mom what we had done. She said, "I am praying that you don't have to go". I knew better than to say anything. During this leave, I began dating Mabel. I walked into my church, Grace Baptist Church, with her on my arm. I did not know that Mary Alice was in the balcony. I was later told she had left the church crying. I had not written or spoken to her since May, when we had the problem in May. I didn't see her when I returned in July or September, either. I know that she attended Norman's funeral, but I don't remember seeing her. I stood up in church, when Reverend Reed, my Pastor, asked for visitors and announcements. I stood up straight and tall in my uniform. Everyone knew who I was, because I had grown up in this church. I informed the congregation that I would be going to Vietnam and asked them for their prayers for a safe return. This was only four months after the funeral for Norman and it was still fresh in everyone's minds. It was very hard for me to perceive just what Norman had been through. I was going to the same place where he had lost his life. I received the well wishes from many people. I was very proud of what I was going to be doing. I was going to serve my country.

I came back home and Mom said that she was still praying that I did not have to go. When she gets on a course, there is no changing it. So, I told her to keep on praying. I knew that I was not going to win this argument. I had to dye all of my white underwear green. Well, that is what I was told to do. Who asks questions? My name was written on my utilities in permanent ink. All of this was done to prepare me to go to Vietnam. I packed my bags and said all of the goodbyes. Mom said again that she was still praying that I did not have to go. We had an early Thanksgiving dinner, because I wouldn't be there for the holiday. It was a very happy time for me and my family. At least, I thought so. My parents had their own nervousness to deal with.

I don't know what was going through my parents minds. Nothing was said about what they were thinking. Dad really didn't say too much to me during this time. I think that he was really scared for me. He never showed any emotions, so this was not unusual for him. He just could not understand why I wanted to fly. I told him flying was what I wanted to do. I was very confident that everything was going to be fine. Everyone from the squadron must have had those same thoughts before their leaving homes and returning to the base. There was no fear on my part. Don't worry about me, I will be alright and coming home when it is over. How can you tell your parents not to worry? Now, that is a real mission impossible. Every parent worries about their children, no matter how old they are or where they go in their life.

These days were going by very fast. Then it happened, it was time to leave. This time, Mom and Dad brought me to the bus station. I checked my bags, while Dad parked his car. He walked slowly towards me. Mom hugged me and said that she was praying that I wouldn't be going. Dad shuck my hand. The thought of this being the last time that I might have seen my parent's faces or their seeing me alive, never entered my mind. I wonder if they had this thought in their minds, as I stepped onto the bus. My parents did not show it, but I think that there were some tears shed by both of them. They were scared for their son's safety and they did not have any control over it. I sat down, smiled and waved goodbye to my parents. The bus pulled off returning me to North Carolina. Their son was going to war.

TRIP TO SOUTHEAST ASIA WITH HMM-262

It was another long bus ride with plenty of time to think. In the back of my mind, I was hoping that my mother's prayers were going to be answered. I knew better and besides this is what I was trained for. I was ready for it. At least, I thought that I was ready. I would later learn that there is no way to prepare a person for the sights and sounds of combat. I got back to the base and we packed up all of our gear. We had been kept so very busy preparing to leave. There was very little time for thinking. There was some nervousness, but then again there was the feeling of excitement and anticipation. Being young and hearing about the combat stories from World War Two, Korea and the traditions of the Marines, this was my chance to be a part of history. This was my chance to serve my country, just like my relatives had done before me.

I was heading for Vietnam, whether I liked it or not. We were leaving by C-130 cargo airplanes. There was some fear, but there was more excitement about Marines going to war. We would show the Viet Cong what it meant to mess with Marines. Well, the weekend was a drunken party. There were beer and wine bottles all over the barracks. The Military Police came to the door and they tried to stop us. They were told, "What are you going to do to us, send us to Vietnam?" We laughed and they left. There really wasn't anything that they could do to the whole squadron. We left a few at a time by buses and rode to the Marine Air Base at Cherry Point, North Carolina, where the transport airplanes were located.

I was on the first airplane out. I got to a phone and called home. Mom answered the phone and I told her that I was leaving. She replied, "I am still praying that you don't have to go." As I looked at the four engine aircraft that was waiting for me, I told her that her prayer didn't work. She needed to start praying that I would get back all right. I told her that

I loved her and I hung up the phone. I didn't think about what was going through my parent's minds at this time. They had been through World War II and the Korean War. They both had seen many people leave home for war. This time it was their own son. I was not trying to worry my parents, but I know that they were. There was nothing that I could do to relieve this feeling. This could be the last time they could have heard my voice. I wasn't thinking about that. Nobody really wants to go to war or fight in a conflict. My Government was sending me. I just stepped onto the airplane, along with my other members of the squadron. The squadron was deploying. It seemed like a normal thing to do. We were trained, now we had a job to do. We were all "Gung Ho" and ready to go.

It was at night, as we rolled down the runway. We took off and headed westward into the black sky. We had typical Marine Corps comfort. The seats were canvas web seats without any cushions. There were a few stretchers strapped up, for beds. All of our gear was stuffed into the plane, along with us. We were packed in like sardines. Well, twelve hours later, we landed at Travis Air Force Base in California. We got out of the plane and they refueled it. We were there for about an hour, just long enough to stretch our legs and it was back into the air. Next stop was the beautiful island of Hawaii for fuel. We landed and got out. It was very warm, but about an hour later we were back in the air. I looked out of one of the windows, as we lifting into the air and saw a palm tree. This was it for Hawaii. It was back over the water and heading west.

It was endless hours of flying over the water, as we soared above the clouds. The pilots of the transport allowed us to go up on the flight deck. Since we were all members of flight crews, there was a mutual understanding between us about the job that they were doing. It was like the pilots were sitting in chairs on a front porch. They had some real comfort. There was a lot more room than in our choppers. Looking out of the cockpit window, the clouds looked like a sea of soft cotton balls and were endless. The navigator showed me a map. He said this is where we are going, while pointing to a speck on the map. It was a tiny dot of land, in the middle of the big blue Pacific Ocean. Out of nowhere, there it was — Wake Island.

We circled this tiny island and landed. We were then informed that there was some engine trouble with our aircraft, so we would be there for a while. It was good to be out of the transport, but on Wake Island, there was nothing there. It was flat, sandy and only a few buildings. There was a radio transmission station there and a hotel for transpacific flight crews. So after getting some chow, we began to explore the island and found it to be beautiful. The water was crystal clear in the small bay. It would have been a fisherman's delight. You could see the white sandy bottom with the fish swimming all around. This was the first time that I had felt the heat under the tropical sun. There was the smell of the warm sea breeze and the sky was a brilliant bright blue. It felt great, especially after the endless hours inside of the transport. Some native children were there and they took us around the island. The warm ocean waters rolled slowly onto the white sandy beach. I found an old bullet that was lying in the sand on the beach. I put it into my pocket and claimed it as a memento of the big war, along with a piece of coral.

I was standing on the beach, looking out to sea. History began to hit me, thinking back to December 7, 1941. I was standing on ground that Marines had fought and died for, twenty-five years earlier, almost to the day. I started to imagine about what it must have been like to wake up in the morning, after Pearl Harbor had been bombed. You are surrounded by a Japanese fleet with no place to run. The highest point on the island was about 20 feet above sea level and there is no place to hide. There was a force of 450 Marines and several hundred civilian workers on the island. They were not going to give up the island without a fight.

We walked along the shore with its white soft sand. The defensive positions of the island were concrete bunkers. They were there from World War II. There were still the bullet holes in them from the battle. I thought about the movie of the battle of Wake Island that had starred William Bendix. This was like I was walking on Hallowed Ground. I had learned about this place in school. I had seen the movie and knew the history. Now here I was standing on that same ground where Marine Corps History was made. This lesson could not be taught in any school. It could only be experienced by standing here. The spirit of the Marine Corps radiated all over this island. The hearts and souls of the Marines Defenders will always be present on this tiny island.

This was the first real battle of the war. I did not see any signs of the enemy naval bombardment of the island that they had endured. The Marines were outnumbered and held off the Japanese forces for several weeks. The enemy had made several attempts to land troops on the island, but were repeatedly repelled. From the continuous naval shelling and overwhelming forces, the Japanese troops landed. The last message received from the Marines on Wake Island stated the Japanese were coming ashore and the situation was in doubt. The Japanese forces took the island after the Marines surrendered it to them. They had fought a good fight and defense. I was overcome with a certain degree of pride and in awe of what those Marines had endured and accomplished. This is what they had been trained to do.

Wake Island Memorial

We walked over to a small monument that was dedicated to the defenders of the island. It had the eagle, globe and anchor on the top of a small steeple along with a plague. Not many people have seen this monument because of it being on this tiny island. The defenders and their sacrifice were not forgotten. I thought about the fears that must have gone through the minds of those defenders with no hope of rescue or reinforcement. Those Marines had fought for this country and the enemy had paid a heavy price. This was Wake Island. I then thought about the pride that had been instilled into us as being Marines and to follow in these defenders footsteps. Would I have the same courage and devotion to duty? I was hoping that I could live up to the traditions of the Marine Corps. Only time would tell.

After about 26 glorious hours in this tropical paradise, our aircraft was fixed. It was back onto the C-130, into the air and over the water, heading west. There was a poker game being played on the rear ramp of the C-130. Well, we hit an air pocket and the plane must have dropped about 500 feet. There were cards, money and several guys floating in the air. Now this was a really floating poker game. The plane regained its lift. Everything hit the ramp and cards were all over the place. We all were floating and shaken up, but no one was hurt. There was a lot of laughing and joking around with the members of the squadron. We were in tight quarters on the flight and there were no signs of nervousness of where we were going.

We made a refueling stop on the island of Guam and went to the chow hall to eat. While we were sitting at a table, everything began to shake. The floor and walls were shaking. It was an earthquake. We ran outside and the ground was still moving. We quickly learned that you can't run away from an earthquake. After a few seconds that seemed like minutes, it was over. It was back into the air and heading for Clark Air Force Base in the Philippines for more fuel and then the flight to South Vietnam. Every stop that we made while crossing the Pacific

Ocean had been fought for during World War II and were a part of history. All of these bases were bought paid for with the blood and lives of Americans from our older generation.

The next stop was at our destination, the Marine Air Base located at Chu Lai, South Vietnam. The sun was shining but I really don't know what time it was, when we landed. We exited the plane and marched onto the white cement flight line. We were well rested, as we had slept most of the time of the flight. There was some confusion, as we unloaded the transport plane that had been our home across the Pacific Ocean. All I knew was the first element of Marine Medium Helicopter Squadron 262 had arrived in Vietnam.

IN-COUNTRY - VIETNAM

We called ourselves, "Bill's Bastards," after our Commanding Officer Lieutenant Colonel William Shadrick. He was a strong leader that had trained and deployed his squadron half way around the world, in less than six months. The squadron's nickname was actually "The Flying Tigers". There was some symbolism of the World War Two "Flying Tigers". Vietnam was the place that we had all read about in the papers and seen on television. It was warm, but nothing like the heat on Wake Island. Things were different here and this was supposed to be a combat zone. We had our rifles, but no ammunition. Some of the guys were looking for the enemy, but there were none to be found. There were sandbags along with other transport and jet aircraft parked on the flight line and ramps. This airport was not much different from the other military airports, with the exception of the sandbags and guard posts protecting the base. Marines worked on the aircraft. Attack aircraft loaded with bombs and rockets. There was the loud roar from the aircraft engines, as they took off from the airstrip, for their missions against the enemy.

We were herded into trucks, along with our duffle bags and left for our base. The unpaved road was bumpy, dirty, and dusty. While en route, one member of the squadron fell off of the back of the truck that he was riding in. He hit his head on the ground and was taken to Clark Air Force Base and we didn't see him again. We weren't in this country for one full day and one of our members was lost to an injury. We arrived at Ky Ha, which was located a few miles north of Chu Lai. This base was where the helicopters were located. We had arrived and were eager to show the enemy what it meant to mess with the Marines. (The enemy was called by many names: Viet Cong — V C — Victor Charlie — Charlie) Sure we were cocky, but we were the best and we would show Charlie how to fight a war. We asked some of the veteran Marines about Charlie. We were told that before we left Vietnam, we would be calling him, Mister Charlie. These were strange words coming from a combat veteran. We thought that we could handle anything.

We received our ammunition and housing assignments. Reality began to hit us; we were actually in Vietnam. It was December 1966. It really didn't take long to get there from the states. We could look out at the South China Sea and the beach. The ground was made up of hard red clay, but the weather was nice. It was not like the hot tropical heat. I felt close to my fellow Marines in the squadron. We were green, as green as we could be, but we were together. We had trained for this together, and we were ready for anything, but we didn't have any combat experience. The other two transport planes arrived. We started getting our living area in order and settling in, so that when our helicopters arrived, we would be ready for action.

The housing was a wooden framed hut with a canvas tent covering the roof, typical Marine comfort. These were called hooches. There was no heat or running water, but we did have electricity. We each had a canvas cot and air mattress that we called a rubber lady. We were issued our pillow, sheets and a blanket. The building with the showers was a short walk from the living area. The bathroom was a whole new adventure, especially to the guys from the city. The outhouses were located near the living area. This was even new to the country boys. The outhouses could accommodate up to six guys at one time. There were no partitions, just six holes in two benches, three on either side. We lost the word privacy very quickly, because there were no single outhouses.

The red clay dust was everywhere and it got into everything. The dust was in the outhouses too. The mess hall was where the food was prepared and served. It was a short walking distance away from the living area and flight line. We had a metal tray with our spoon, fork, knife and canteen cup. After eating, there were two garbage cans. One can was filled with hot soapy boiling water and the other had clean boiling water. Everything was strung together with string or wire. We would dip the eating utensils into one can and then the other. It was a quick way of doing the dishes. We had all that was needed, at least for Marines.

Here I was a Jet Helicopter Mechanic, a qualified Crew Chief, Port Side Gunner and ready to fly, but I did not have a helicopter. Our pilots and some of the other Crew Chiefs began flying with the other squadrons that were already in-country. They were getting the experience that was needed for flying in combat. I knew that my turn would come. In my case, I was assigned to guard duty. Others were assigned to mess duty and others were checking the other equipment that we had brought with us. I found myself pulling interior guard duty, during the night. We would walk the mat of the flight line, where the helicopters were parked and the living area. It was very dark and quiet. We strained to hear or see anything moving in the darkness. The smells of the JP-4 jet fuel and hydraulic fluid were the same, only more intense. The night was very dark, with the exception for some lights in the tent area. I guess that everything was more sensitive. Protection of the choppers was our main concern. They were vital to our mission in this country.

It began to rain, and then it was pouring rain. No one told us this was the monsoon season. This meant continuous days of rain, their rainy season. The red clay soon turned into red mud. It was thick and like glue. Walking to the showers in the morning was an adventure, as we were slipping and sliding on the mud. The sun was gone, and it was raining almost every day. The canvas roof of our hooch began to leak. Needless to say everything was either damp or wet. When it wasn't raining, there were low gray clouds almost down to the ground. Somebody also turned off the heat too. It was very chilly. Life and the war still went on.

One night, I was walking guard around the helicopter mat in the rain. It was miserable. There was another Marine guard with his dog. He told me to watch this. He put his helmet on the dog and put a cigar into the dog's mouth and walked away. The dog didn't move. He walked to the far end of the tar mat and called the dog and he came on a dead run. Well, one night this guy fell into a ditch along the side of the mat and was injured. The dog would not let anyone near him to help him. It was morning before they could get another dog handler there, so that we could help him. Walking the helicopter mat in the dark had plenty of dangers.

By this time, I was going on patrols, just outside of the base. I heard the sound of a chopper and looked up. A CH-34 helicopter was flying over head. I began to wonder about what I was doing on the ground. I was supposed to be flying and I wasn't a grunt. I was in the shallow rice paddies and bushes that surrounded the base. We were looking for any evidence of the Viet Cong being around the perimeter during the night. A Marine is a rifleman first, but not me. I was supposed to be flying. It was strange, but I did the job. Talk about a fish out of water, which is what I felt like.

Vietnamese civilians were working on the base. Some of them were members of the Viet Cong, but which ones were the enemy? Men, women and children came through the gates every morning. There were no uniforms on this enemy. They washed our clothes and cleaned different areas on the base. When the attacks came at night, the mortars and rockets were very accurate. Some of these workers had carefully mapped out the base for the enemy. We learned to reposition the choppers after the civilians left the base at the end of the day.

The middle of December 1966 came and so did our helicopters. The members of our squadron that were aboard the ship couldn't wait to get their feet on solid ground again. They had been at sea for over a month. The ship was in sight, just off the coast. We went aboard and got the planes ready for the short flight to the base at Ky Ha. We were the third CH-46 squadron to be deployed in-country. HMM-164 had been the first and was stationed at the Marble Mountain Air Base, just outside of DaNang. They had problems with the sand and dirt getting into the engines. We were equipped with engine dust filters and we were ready.

The helicopters flew onto the base and they were beautiful. The big powerful jet engine choppers, shining from their dark green paint, were parked on the helio pad, next to the CH-34's, which were well worn and a dirty faded green paint. Our choppers had a bigger lifting capacity, speed and range. They were armed with M-60 machine guns for protection, but they were soon changed to the .50 caliber machine guns. The larger guns had more knockdown power. Charlie would shoot back when the M-60 was fired at them, but would hide when the 50's opened up. Now the squadron was in Vietnam for real.

They began flight operations from the first day that the choppers were there. There was a sense of pride among us. We had moved an entire squadron from the East Coast of the United States to this far off land in about a month. The Squadron call letters were E T, pronounced Echo Tango, and painted on each chopper in black. HMM - 262 had arrived and was an operational squadron. I said they were flying, because I was still on the ground.

One night, it was real late and raining very hard. One of the Marines went into his hooch and a shot rang out. Another member of the squadron had shot him. The bullet passed just behind his eyes. He was medevaced and we never saw him again. The next incident took place in my hooch. I was lying on my cot, and there was a guy across from me. He had been cleaning his M-14 rifle and was checking the magazine. The rifle was lying across his lap and he was ejecting the rounds.

The magazine carried twenty bullets. He was counting them, as he ejected them from the rifle. He popped the safety off and pulled the trigger. There was a loud bang, as the rifle went off. Who said that Marines were smart and could count to twenty! The bullet struck the guy in the cot next to me in the foot. The bullet ripped through his flesh and went through the canvas tent and into the next hooch. It narrowly missed a guy's head, while he was sitting on his cot reading a book.

My wounded hooch mate next to me sat up and looked at his foot. His big toe was hanging by a small piece of meat. He asked me for a cigarette. After a few drags, he laid back down, while first aid was given to him. He did not say anything, I guess that he was in a state of shock. I know that I was. I saw just what a bullet could do to a body for the first time. Before this, we only shot at paper targets, this time it was flesh. The bullet had ripped open his skin on his foot and continued on its way. He was medevaced and I never saw him again either. We had been in-country less than a month and three members of the squadron had been injured. We had not seen or heard from the enemy. Not one of their injuries was due to the actions of the enemy. This is what happens when everyone has bullets and is green to combat. Life could be very dangerous. We had lost three Marines due to our own accidents.

Then came more reality. There were many nights that you would lie down and fall asleep, just to be awakened by the sound of the siren going off and the sounds of boom, boom, boom. It would be the sound of mortar rounds or rockets exploding and impacting on the base. Someone would yell, "IN COMING." It was only said once. Everyone would grab their rifles and would be on a dead run for the protection of the sandbagged bunkers. We huddled in the darkness of the bunkers and we were scared. The explosions would get closer. The ground and sandbagged wall shook and dust filled the air from the force of the blasts. Most of the explosives were aimed at the helicopters, which were more important than us and a lot harder to replace, but some were landing in the living area. There was always the wondering of where the next explosion might be.

Now, this is combat. Your nerves were always on edge, blood pressure rising, but this was not every night. Every time you would get comfortable and could get some sleep, there were the explosions to bring you back to reality. After a few times of being hit, you learned to leave your rifle in the hooch. It only got in the way while running and diving into the bunker. If Charlie was coming through the base, there was plenty of time to get your rifle. There were exterior guard posts, bunkers and interior guard posts. Charlie overrunning the base never entered our minds. He didn't want to try that either, because we were ready for him. We were scared, but ready. This didn't stop the mortars and rockets being sent to remind us that they were still out there.

After the day's work was done, it was off to the enlisted mens club and there was the beer. We drank a lot of beer. There were Tiger beer, Falstaff, Black Label, and others. They all were 3.2 beers, this meant that the alcohol content was only 3.2%. You could drink a gallon of it, but we were young and you could get drunk. It took your mind off of the war and what was going on around you.

Another fellow Marine was Joseph "Jake" Jacobs. We had trained together and now we were in Vietnam. We were sitting on top of a bunker, watching flares and gunfire off in the distance. Jake turned to me and asked, "What do the colored people think about the war?" I stopped him right there and asked him, "What color am I?" He replied that I was Black. I told him that's right, I am not colored. Jake was embarrassed. He said that he had never been around Black People until joining the Marines. He was raised in Wisconsin and there weren't many black people there. We talked for quite a while about life in general. Jake was totally honest about his education and growing up. His Mother would have never allowed him to think that he was any better than anyone else. He learned the same about me. There was a lot of learning, on both our parts, that night. We both received an education that night. We became even closer and to this day, I still respect him for his honesty and his friendship.

Here it was my first Christmas in Vietnam 1966; in fact, it would be my first Christmas ever being away from home and my family. It felt very strange not to be surrounded by family and friends that I had grown up with. There was turkey dinner being served in the mess hall, with a little decorated Christmas tree. The smells weren't those of Mom's cooking, but the food was filling. Christmas carols were being played on the radio from the Armed Forces Radio. This could not be Christmas, there was no snow and it was raining. It was definitely not a Christmas in Connecticut.

The squadron was up and running. I was working on the flight line as a mechanic. There were plenty of injuries that happened to the mechanics while working around the machinery. There were cuts from the safety wire and cotter pins that held the aircraft together, along with the bruises, busted knuckles and lumps from tools that slipped, as well as losing your awareness of working around moving parts. There was the slipping and falling on the oily surfaces. These injuries were taken in stride, as they were all just part of the job of a mechanic and keeping the choppers flying. I still did not have a helicopter to call my own and zero flight time in combat.

Several choppers came back from missions with bullet holes in them. I guess this was war. We would hear the stories of the resupply or troop transport missions, not to mention being shot at or carrying the wounded. There was excitement amongst the flight crews. They were doing their job. Being a part of the ground crew wasn't exciting. We did our job to keep the choppers flying.

New Year's Eve came and it was also strange. All was quiet until midnight came, there was firing around the perimeter and pop up flares being shot into the air. It was their way of saying, "Hello 1967!" We were on high alert because it was figured that the V.C. might attack. Nothing happened that night, but our way of celebrating the new year coming in.

Jake reminded me years later of one night in Vietnam. We had been drinking and we went to the enlisted men's club at Ky Ha. Whose idea it was has faded from my memory, but we came up with a plan. We entered the club. As usual, the Blacks Marines were on one side and the White Marines were on the other. There was country and western being played on one side and soul music on the other. Needless to say, which side was which. Well, Jake headed for the Country music and turned it up. I went the other way and turned up the soul music. I yelled at him to turn off that hillbilly music. He in turn shouted to me to turn off the cotton picking music. The entire club got deadly quiet. I told Jake to make me turn off the music and we slowly walked toward the middle of the club. We were still mouthing at each other and began approaching each other.

Everyone else in the club got very quiet and was watching to see what was going to happen. I balled up my fists, as did Jake. When we got to within arm length of each other, we swung at each other. Our arms surrounded each other and we hugged each other. We started laughing. Well both sides of the club came together and grabbed both of us. They threw us out of the club. We landed in the mud, while they threw empty beer cans at us. We were rolling in the mud, while trying to stand up and still laughing. This really broke the ice, and there were never any serious problems. It was a very funny joke that we played on all of them.

We were drunk and crawled to our hooch. We were covered with red mud and fell into our cots, with our clothes on and fell asleep. In the morning, Jake and I went to take a shower. Someone asked us about what we thought of the mortar attack. We replied, "What attack?" The guy said the mortar attack last night. Jake and I had slept through the entire attack. I guess that God does take care of Drunks and Fools. Well, he certainly had his hands full with us.

January 1967, reality came to the cocky members of the squadron. I was working on the flight line. The morning flights were launched as usual. The word came that someone had been hit on one of our choppers. Our minds began racing like crazy. Who was it and how bad were they hurt? There was a nervous tension that ran throughout the squadron. We soon learned it was Sergeant Clarence I. Henry, a Crew Chief that was hit. He had extended his enlistment to deploy to Vietnam, with the squadron. We never saw him again. He had been killed. His chopper and crew came back, but he didn't. He was taken directly to the hospital. He was the first member of the squadron to die in combat, but he would not be the last.

The story of what had happened began to flow. While flying on a mission, his chopper came under ground fire. He had been hit in the face by a bullet that had passed through the chopper. There were a few traces of blood in the cabin area. The papers that had contained the bandages used to treat him were on the floor of his helicopter. C. I. was dead and gone, just like that!

The reality of war had come to HMM-262. Certainly, there were the fun and games. We had arrived as a squadron and we were close. We said nobody dies and we all go home. This was the serious side of doing our business and you could get killed. You could be here in the morning and then gone forever. The loss was very hard to take. Not only was he a friend and a Marine, but he was Black. This fact had nothing to do with his death, but he was older than the rest of us young kids in the squadron. He was like the older brother that was always looking out for the rest of us.

There was a high degree and deep sense of loss. First of all, we had to believe that it was true. Everyone was walking around in a daze and a state of shock. We had laughed with him the night before. He got up and took off in his chopper for his mission. Everything was normal, but he did not come back. Secondly, his chopper was there and so was his cot in his hooch, but his bubbly attitude and smile were now gone forever. We tried not to think about the loss of C. I., but you could not help it. C. I.'s life had come to an abrupt end. This fact of life hit us very hard. How do you grieve for the loss of a fellow Marine? No one had ever taught us about this, but we would have to live with the fact that he was gone. He would not be forgotten. The war went on and the squadron continued doing its job, flying missions and supporting our troops.

BINGO --- REALITY CHECK --- YOU CAN GET KILLED DOING THIS JOB!!!

HELICOPTER SQUADRON - HMM-164 "FLYING DEATH"

The month of February 1967 came and so did word that there was going to be transfers to other squadrons. Our squadron was too green and inexperienced. We needed combat experienced Marines. The replacements would be brought in from other helicopter squadrons, to bring our squadron up to fighting strength. Now the wondering began again. Who was going and who was staying? I was a Crew Chief, and they needed me. I wasn't going anywhere. I had trained and deployed with this squadron, this was my family and I wasn't going anywhere. I couldn't have been more wrong.

I learned that I would be going to HMM-164, which was located at the helicopter base at Marble Mountain. This base was further north and along the coast. Here I was with not one minute of flight time in combat and leaving my friends. I did not get a chance to prove myself to the ones that I had trained with. I felt like I was letting them down. How do you just walk away? I really didn't want to go, but those were the orders. I was not the only one leaving the squadron. About twenty of us were heading to a new home. Before it was over, half of the squadron would be transferred to different squadrons.

It was a quick goodbye to those I had trained and deployed with. We loaded our gear into a chopper and jumped in for the short flight to our new base. It was strange arriving at the new squadron HMM-164. I was the "Nicky New Guy", also known as the FNG (Fucking New Guy). This squadron had been in country for almost a year and they were salty. They were proud, but not cocky. They had been through the testing of the CH-46 chopper in combat. Part of their squadron had been transferred to 262. I know they did not want to leave their friends either.

The Marble Mountain Air Facility (MMAF) was a much larger base as compared to Ky Ha. The living area with its' hooches was better than the ones in Ky Ha. We were still sleeping on cots. The flight line was about the same, but there were better buildings. The buildings were open air with no air conditioning. They were just shelters for the choppers, while they were being repaired. The support buildings were wooden frames with tin roofs. There were several other helicopter squadrons stationed at the MMAF, but they had the CH-34's, Hueys and CH-37's. The choppers were dirty and looked well worn, nothing like our brand new ones that we had brought with 262. At the far end of the flight line was the Bone Yard. This is where the wrecked helicopters laid twisted and broken. Some of the choppers were shot down and brought back, while others were hit by rockets or mortar explosions on the base. These aircraft would never fly again, but there were plenty of parts that could be used on other choppers. We were located a few miles outside the City of DaNang, with its large Air Force Base. We checked in and were given our assignments. We settled in and began to get acquainted with our new squadron mates.

I was the New Guy in the squadron and a little nervous. They didn't know anything about me. I would have to pick up on their experience and learn about life in combat. There were no strangers in combat, just friends that I haven't met yet. Conversations started whenever two guys got together. We spread the news from home and talked about the things that the veterans had missed from being so far away. It was my turn to join them in their struggle to survive..

The makeup of HMM-164 was the same, about 250 Marines with very few Blacks; there was one Officer and a couple of Crew Chiefs. There were some mechanics, avionics, transportation and metal shop personnel that were minorities. Could we have been special? I don't think so. We were no smarter than anyone else. I guess that we were just luckier. We had the knowledge and the opportunity to demonstrate our skills. This did not bother me, because I never looked at people by their color. To me, we were all Marines. I also now was wondering, why there were so few minorities in the air wing? I must admit that I felt a sense of pride whenever I saw another Black Crew Chief or Pilot. I knew what they had gone through to obtain their positions. They were few and far between. To see a Crew Chief or a Pilot at the controls of the helicopter who was Black must have shocked some people, but there was never any question of their ability.

The Pilots, Crew Chiefs and Gunners were the high profile jobs in the Marine Squadron. I said high profile jobs, because every job is important to the operation of the squadron. The Administrative, Supply, Support and Motor Transport Sections, along with the Chaplain were all essential to getting the choppers in the air. They all tried to keep us together physically, mentally and spiritually. When that didn't work, there was always the universal substitute for worrying, which is women and booze. They were not hard to find.

This squadron was like all the others and had its own share of characters. There were the comical, the serious and those that were just plain crazy. This was the same for the Officers, as well as the Enlisted personnel. This was an easygoing outfit. Everyone was greasy and dirty, with a laid back attitude. When it was time for work, they worked hard. When it was time to party, they partyed hardy. This was a new attitude for me, because before this it was all strictly military. I guess that you could call this a combat attitude. One thing was for sure, they all knew their jobs. There was a strong sense of loyalty to each other and to the mission of supporting the troops.

I began working as a mechanic on the flight line and still no chopper to fly. I was servicing the choppers that needed work. There were engines and transmissions to change, along with changing parts that had high flight time on them. We changed oil and greased all of the moving parts, just like working on a car. There was the repairing of battle damage. Many choppers were hit by bullets and shrapnel from explosions. We worked like busy bees putting them back together.

I would have taken the crew position of being a gunner on any flight. This would have given me some combat flight experience, but that was not to be. My mind wandered. I was thinking about my friends that I missed and had left with HMM-262. I knew what they were doing and where they were, but how were they really doing? They were flying around the Chu Lai area, supporting our Marines, the South Vietnamese Army and the South Korean Marines.

Being a qualified Crew Chief, I was issued my flight equipment that included a flight suit, gloves, helmet, survival knife and emergency flares. I would be flying and hoped that it would be sooner than later. The problem was when? I was ready, willing and eager to fly, but I needed a helicopter.

FIRST COMBAT MISSION

Early one morning, a guy wearing a flight suit approached me, while I was walking to the flight line. He asked me if I was a qualified crew chief and I told him that I was. He then asked me if I had a chopper and I replied, "No". He asked me if I wanted one and I told him, YES! He said that I could take his chopper on a flight. My eyes were popping out and my heart was racing. For the first time, I was being given the chance to prove myself. He asked me if I had a screwdriver and I said no. He handed me his. He then said here is my .38 caliber pistol and six bullets. I headed for the flight line and his helicopter. He went back to the hooch area and must have thought that I was crazy or some kind of a nut. I guess I was grinning for ear to ear, while trying to look like a professional. I was 19 years old and would be responsible for a CH-46, a million dollar transport helicopter, and it was going to be my baby. I had passed the tests, watched the choppers takeoff and return, heard the stories about the flights and now it was time for the practical application in combat. It was my turn to prove myself. My dream was going to come true.

I grabbed my flight equipment and walked steadily to the flight line with a sense of confidence. There was also a bit of nervousness inside of me, as I approached the helicopter. I looked at this big green flying machine with a sense of pride. It was dirty and its paint was a dull green. This aircraft would be my first chopper in Vietnam. It was mine, at least for now. The flight had been scheduled and I did my pre-flight inspection of the chopper. It is the Crew Chief's responsibility to say whether or not the chopper is flight worthy. I checked the engines, the transmissions, drive train, the rotor heads and all of the systems. The plexiglass windows in the cabin were broken out and the interior insolation had been removed, but that was all right. Everything mechanical was right. I went to the line shack and signed the yellow sheet in the log book for

65

the chopper (this meant that I said the chopper was ready for flight).

My gunner arrived with the two .50 caliber machine guns. We mounted them into the chopper and checked the ammunition. I guess that he knew I was green, because of my very clean green flight suit and this was my first flight. I was the rookie of this crew, but you have to learn at sometime. I guess that my excitement was showing. My two pilots arrived and after checking the aircraft over, I secured the inspection hatches. We were ready to go. The pilots crawled into the cockpit and took their seats. They told me we would be flying up to Khe Sanh for some resupply missions. Khe Sanh, I had never heard of this place, but I was ready for anything.

I put on my bullet bouncer. This body armor consisted of a front and back plate, made out of laminated fiberglass. It was held together by shoulder straps and two Velcro straps around your waist. It weighed about twenty pounds. They said that it would stop just about any bullet. I strapped on my .38 pistol, put on my helmet and plugged into the Inter-aircraft Communications System (ICS). I adjusted my lip microphone and the pilot began to talk to me through the ICS. After going through the prestart checklist, the pilot was ready to fire up the Auxiliary Power Plant (APP). This small jet engine provided electrical and hydraulic power to the chopper to start the engines. He said, "Ready on the APP?" I replied, "Ready on the APP." I was holding the fire extinguisher in the event of a fire. The pilot hit the switch. There was a small whine and it fired off and began running. I then walked to the number one engine. The pilot radioed, "Ready on One?" and I replied, "Ready on One". With this, the pilot took the engine control lever and moved it to the crank position. The number one jet engine began to whine, as it was rotating by the hydraulic starter. There was a strong smell of jet fuel before it fired off and began running. The heat from the jet exhaust hit me in the face. I was standing too close to the exhaust. I was standing in the wrong spot. No one else had seen this, but I knew better. My nervousness was showing. I walked to the other side of the chopper. The next request was "Ready on Two?" and I replied, "Ready on Two." It began running. I went inside the cabin and closed the ramp. I then went out the cabin door to the front of the chopper, while the pilots went through their preflight checklist and to give me a thumbs up signal. This meant that everything was okay. I returned this signal.

I signaled the pilot that it was clear to engage and start the rotor blades. The pilot disengaged the rotor brake which held the rotor blades stationary. He pushed the engine control levers to the fly position and the engines began to rev up. The six big rotor blades began turning. The helicopter started to rock from side to side, as the blades turned slowly. The chopper was coming to life. It settled down, as the blades turned faster and faster, getting up to the normal operating speed. I jumped in, locking the cabin door behind me. We began taxiing down the flight line for the runway. There were two helicopters in this flight and we followed our wingman onto the runway.

While we were taxiing, I was listening to the sounds of the aircraft and checking the gauges in the cockpit. The helicopter has certain sounds that will let you know that everything is okay. There was the high pitched whine of the jet engines, the warming hums of the transmissions and the popping of the rotor blades. Together these sounds were in harmony. It was like music and the machine was operating smoothly. The Crew Chief is aware to every sound.

I glanced at and checked the Master Caution Panel located between the pilots in the center of the instrument panel in the cockpit. This panel contained the warning lights for conditions that could endanger the flight. All of the lights were out and everything was fine. The pilots sat up front and trusted their gauges, while the Crew Chief also listened for sounds that might indicate a problem that might not be covered by a gauge.

I sat down in the Crew Chief's jump seat located just behind the cockpit and tried to relax. My gunner took his position at his machine gun on the left side of the chopper. We rolled onto the runway and the pilot pulled in power. The chopper took off and lifted into the air. We flew down the runway, slowly gaining altitude. My heart was really racing now! This whole procedure would be repeated hundreds of times. With each and every flight, the feeling was always the same. There is a certain excitement about flying, along with some sense of apprehension of what could happen, but this thought never really entered my mind. We were invincible. I was a Marine, in combat, and a member of a flight crew. This is what I had been trained for; a Helicopter Crew Chief flying in combat. I was actually doing it!

Crew Chief

The pilot headed our chopper for the South China Sea and turned north. The pilot said to lock and load. This meant to arm the machine guns, of which we did. It was safer to fly over the water, a few miles off of the coast. This way, Charlie couldn't take any pot shots at us. I put my Mae West life preserver on under my bullet bouncer, just in case we went down in the water. My swimming had not improved, but I was a second class swimmer. I sat in the jump seat by the cabin door and looked out at the waves of the South China Sea, lapping at the white sandy beaches. The villages of Vietnam and the landscape were very pretty. This country would be like a resort, if it wasn't for the war. The landscape was flat and a bright green from the foliage of the countryside. The air was cleaner while flying, as the wind blew through the cabin. There was a sense of freedom of being in another dimension, as I looked out of the cabin door at the world below or the rear hatch of the chopper. All of the flight systems were functioning properly. I had an enormous sense of pride and responsibility. My chopper was flying and I was its' Crew Chief!

I later learned that taking off from Marble Mountain and heading north, the first big river inlet was Phu Bai, while the second one was Dong Ha, and the third river was North Vietnam, which was no man's land. It sounded like an easy way to navigate. We were operating in the I Corp area of the country, which was the northern most part of Vietnam. We flew missions from the South China Sea to the borders of Cambodia and Laos to the Demilitarized Zone (DMZ) in the north separating North and South Vietnam, as well as everywhere in between.

My mind began racing. I did not know what was going to happen next. Would I be able to perform my duties under fire? What would happen if we were shot at? I never thought about being shot down, being down in the field, wounded or even being killed. I watched the gauges in the cockpit and listened to every sound of the chopper, as we headed north.

I was responsible for this helicopter. I was in charge of the cabin section and the right side machine gunner. Yes, there were some fears and nervousness, but I had my job to do. I knew that I had an obligation to my crew. I had something to prove, not only to myself, but also to the other members of my crew and the Marine Corps. There was an inner feeling of importance being part of a flight crew. This was my first combat flight in Vietnam and being in charge of my own helicopter. I was really excited!

We reached the base at Dong Ha. The pilots turned west and headed inland over the beaches. We passed two large mountains, the Rockpile and the Razorback. The Rockpile was a mountain that rose up from the valley floor to about 700 feet and there was a Marine observation post located there. We headed up a long valley and there was our objective, the base at Khe Sanh. It was situated on a mesa surrounded by mountains, close to the Laotian border in the northwest corner of Vietnam. This outpost was vital to the running of military operations. It was like being out on a limb, Hell's Half Acre. We landed on the small runway and taxied to the helicopter parking area. We shut the aircraft down. The pilots went for their briefing, while I checked the chopper over.

Upon the pilots' return, I learned that it was going to be a resupply mission. I configured the interior of the chopper from carrying passengers to hauling cargo. We got to work. We flew to the resupply area (Landing Zone or Loading Zone, known as the L Z) and loaded the chopper with ammunition, water, C-rations (food), along with anything else the troops in the field needed. I directed the Marines on how to load the chopper, making sure of the weight and balance, along with the security of the load. Off we went. Our chopper lifted up and headed for the L Z. We landed where this delivery was scheduled and they unloaded the cargo. It was back into the air for a return flight to the Loading Zone for another load. We flew many resupply missions the entire day, while bringing back some wounded Marines to the first aid station at Khe Sanh.

This was the highland region of Vietnam. The mountains were covered in green foliage and the hills were beautiful. We knew that the V. C. was under the jungle canopy somewhere. Where were they? We flew from one outpost to another, bringing in the supplies. After several trips, we were running low on fuel. We landed at the fuel dump. It was like a gas station, as we taxied up to the next available hose. I got out and filled the chopper with hundreds of gallons of the JP 4 jet fuel. We then flew to the loading area and the next flight. At the end of the day, to my surprise, we did not return to Marble Mountain, but stayed in the hooches at Khe Sanh. We slept and ate with the Marines stationed there. I learned to appreciate what the Grunts had to go through. There were mortar and rocket attacks. We were in and out of the bunkers on a regular basis.

Red clay and red dust covered the mesa. There were hot days and cold nights. The choppers blew the dust everywhere. During the monsoon season, the dust turned to red glue (commonly known as mud). The thick gooey, slippery, messy red mud was everywhere. It did not snow, but it got really cold. In the morning, there was a mist that surrounded the valley and the base. Fog presented the most dangerous type of flying. Low visibility, mountains and the loss of ground reference points kept everyone on edge, but the flights went on. I don't have the slightest idea of how many missions were flown, but there were a lot. There were numerous sorties (flights back and forth to the same zone). Each day and night, I would check the chopper over, making any necessary repairs. There is a lot of maintenance that has to be performed to keep the bird flying. We stayed there for almost two weeks, before we headed back to our base. This was my first flight and the first of many trips into the base at Khe Sanh.

Although my squadron was stationed at Marble Mountain, we had choppers assigned to the bases at Khe Sanh and Dong Ha. This gave us a faster response to the troops. There were emergencies that would pop up at any time; such as search and rescue, medevac and resupply missions.

Flying back to MMAF, we were dirty and smelly. We did not have a shower the entire time that we were gone. My flight suit was now greasy and dirty, because I did not have a change of clothing. Needless to say the rest of me was the same. It is funny, when everyone around you is the same, no one is any different.

After we parked the chopper, shut it down, and checked it over. I walked slowly toward the hooch area. I then looked over and there stood the same guy that had given me his chopper. He was laughing. I said to him, "Are you a Crew Chief?" He replied yes. I asked him if he had a chopper and he said no. Well, we went though the same routine that he had given me. I gave him back his chopper. He had gone on Rest and Recuperation (R& R). He knew the mission was going to be for at least a week. I was tired and went to my hooch and fell into my rack. I continued to work on the flight line as a mechanic and took flights, when a chopper was available. The ice had been broken. I was a Combat Flying Crew Chief and it felt good.

COMBAT CREWS

Being off of the ground at anytime brings about its own perils. Flying has its own dangers; in a helicopter only makes it even more dangerous by flying low and slow and then add in the enemy that is trying to shoot you down. It all adds up to a very nerve racking, hair-raising and tension packed life. We actually thrived on the pressure of this life style. There was an ever growing sense of pride and of accomplishment being a member of a flight crew. There never a shortage of Crew Chiefs or Gunners willing to take a flight. The Marines on the ground needed us and we would be there for them. We had the reputation of going anywhere and whenever we were needed. The job was the mission and no job was too difficult. We painted the big white YT (our call letters) high on the aft (rear) pylon, and it was a welcome sight to the Grunts on the ground.

On Friday, March 13th, they had scheduled me to fly on chopper YT-13, pronounced Yankee Tango 13. I was not superstitious, but the guys were making me that way. The Crew Chiefs joked about how unlucky the number was. They had made me nervous about flying on this chopper. So, I loaded the chopper with 1,300 rounds of ammunition and thirteen grenades. We took off and completed our missions. It turned out to be a very uneventful day. Each and every Crew Chief had his own little quirks that would bring some luck. No one ever talked about them, but we all had our own little rituals before each and every flight. A little extra luck never hurt.

I was later assigned YT-14, as my regular chopper. My helicopter was like a girlfriend and I loved it just as much. Every Crew Chief had the same feelings about their aircraft. We had to know everything about it as we tended to them and cared for their every need. You take care of her and she will take care of you. My life and the lives of those onboard depended on my chopper. It needed plenty of attention, just like a woman.

The Jet Jockeys or the Fast Movers, also known as the fighter pilots, bomber pilots and their crews had a different prospective of combat. The crews of the Huey Cobras and Huey Gun Ships had still another view of this war. Their views were very impersonal. They would fly in close, fire or drop their ordinance and then it was back into the safety of skies. We were glad to have their support and the protection from their added firepower. The artillery at the firebases would send shells of explosives in support of the troops. They were never up close and personal, but they all had their own pressures to deal with. Kill the enemy and protect our troops. We all shared the fears of being hit at night. We controlled the day, while Charlie came out of hiding and ruled the night. Charlie picked his place and time to attack us. The V C could be anywhere.

Being in a transport helicopter is a different type of flying and prospective of combat. Most people never even think about the 4-man crew that it takes to operate this complex flying machine called a helicopter. Bring together four individuals of different ages, from all around the country and train them. They all have come from different backgrounds and cultures, but have to perform as a crew. Each person has a job to do and has to function as a team. The only things that they have in common were that they are Americans and Marines. This is all that mattered. It was an unspoken slogan - "You Call, We Haul". Whatever it took to complete the mission, was done. The troops needed something and the choppers brought it. Flight after flight, mission after mission, L Z after L Z, day and night; the flight crews had to deal with this constant pressure. The concern for their own personal safety, even unconsciously, went from one battle area to another.

In our case, we were on the ground with the troops. We saw their faces with the dirt and sweat dripping off, as well as their wounds. We felt their pains. Our emotions were with them from the time that we picked them up, the long ride to the L Z, dropping them off and bringing them back home. Flight after flight, the faces changed but their expressions were always the same. There was a blank stare, a look of fear and doubt of going into combat and a sense of relief on the return flights. The pressures of going into the unknown and performing their jobs was always on their minds. The flight crews felt these same pressures, as we were doing the same thing. Our job was to complete the mission, no matter what it was. There were also the thoughts of what was ahead of us with each takeoff and what could be waiting for us to arrive? The thoughts were there, to keep us alert, but there was no worrying about it.

There was never any nervousness about the flight itself. We had been trained as Marines and in the maintenance of the helicopter. Every Crew Chief knows about the danger signs and conditions that could endanger the flight. The inspections of the mechanical, electronic and hydraulic systems were done. Test flights were flown and the chopper was ready. Flying was the job and we were ready. What an awesome responsibility for any 19 - 20 year old to have!

We were the riders, while the pilots were the drivers. They sat up front and had the job of getting us in and out of some of the most difficult terrain on Earth. The Crew Chief watched every landing, as the pilots could not see the rear of the chopper and cleared us to land. We hopped from one landing zone to another, delivering whatever was needed. Wherever the Grunts went, we would follow supporting them. With each mission, there was a degree of nervousness of what we could be running into. On any flight, we could find ourselves in the middle of a firefight and a battle could be raging at any time.

We would be flying into the teeth of the battle and the chopper was a very big tempting target to the enemy.

There was also a heightened sense of excitement, while we were flying between the trees, landing in the rice paddies or in the elephant grass that could stand several feet high, or even perched on a mountaintop. We were ever vigilant looking for the enemy. They could see and hear the chopper long before we could see them. We were a big inviting target. Suddenly there would be rifles firing and seeing the muzzles flashes, as they were firing the bullets at us. The response was in an instant and without thinking; swing the machine gun onto the target and press the trigger. The gun came alive, spraying bullets in the direction of the flashes. The enemy fire stopped shooting, at least until we departed the area. Our troops would engage the enemy in a battle, but for us it was different. We were flying from one battle zone and into another.

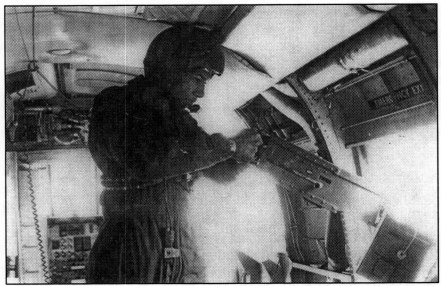

Gunner --- inside of chopper with .50 cal machine gun.

The port (left) side gunner was also Marine, who could be a mechanic or other squadron support personnel. He was a qualified aerial gunner, seated in the cabin section with his machine gun. His job was to protect the left side of the chopper. He would also assist the Crew Chief in some of his duties. When the gunner was not flying, he would be doing his regular job in the squadron. Being a gunner was another voluntary assignment. There was never a shortage of those willing to fly.

Our evenings were full of reading and writing letters, listening to music, drinking and trying to rest after a day of flights and maintenance work on our birds. There was just too much time for thinking. There were few thoughts about back home. Letters flowed back and forth across the ocean on a regular basis. Reading the words from those that loved you or at least cared about you was a pleasant relief after the endless hours of work. There were people back in the world having fun. They did not have to spend their time in Hell or be treated like someone that had dropped off the face of the Earth. Birthdays, anniversaries and holidays came and went without much attention. The only anniversary that meant anything was the date that you were going home. We were just existing and made our own fun and games with the little free time that we had.

Thinking about what we had done and missing our friends that had lost their lives were always on our minds. We thought about the round eyed women back in the world, and missing a life that was so far away. Reading Playboy magazines and seeing the pictures inside helped us to remember what we were fighting for and what we missed. The mental pressure was always there, but we had a job to do. We had to deal with this pressure on a daily basis. The emotional ups and downs were constant and we learned to live with them. The threat of Charlie hitting us with rockets and mortars at night was always there. How much of this life style was a person supposed to be

77

able to take? We really didn't dwell on the others that had died, even though they were missed. We knew that other Americans were dying every day in this country called Vietnam.

Each morning was the same. We would get up early, have breakfast and it was onto the flight line. If the choppers were not flight worthy, we would work on them and make them flyable. If the aircraft were in an up status (ready to fly), we would preflight the choppers and we were ready. The pilots got their briefings for the day's missions and arrived at our choppers, with their maps and clipboards in hand. We would be then taking off for the day's work. The choppers carried us in and out of harm's way, only being controlled by the skill of the pilots. Upon returning to the base at the end of the day, it was more working on the chopper to have it ready to fly again. The next morning, it would be the same thing all over again. This routine was anything but a rut. No two days were the same. There was always something to be done.

The helicopter pilots were a different breed of Marine. They strutted with nerves of steel. They were good at what they were doing. The pilots had their own fears of sitting up in front, without much protection. A helicopter is not an easy machine to fly. The pilots had the ability to coordinate the collective, cyclic and rudder controls, along with the power just to get the chopper off the ground. They had an air of confidence about themselves, their abilities and in their flight crew that the mission would be completed. The Marine Officers, who were the pilots, also gained a respect for the Crew Chiefs and their abilities. Some pilots were as crazy as we were and they were good. We could fly to Hell and back with good pilots. All of the pilots were not like that and we knew who the better ones were. The pressure and tension levels were always high and intense.

We knew the dangers of flying with each and every takeoff, but the hazards never stopped us. There was a job to do and we had the responsibility of being there for the troops. Nothing is totally safe. There was never a relief from the pressure of flying in combat. We had to learn to live with that pressure, making life and death decision every day with our work. Nothing in life will age you faster than living in combat. Young men were growing very old, very quickly, day by day.

When we transported the troops or cargo and the temperature of the air dictated the number of troops or how much cargo, in other words, the amount of weight that we could carry. The cooler the temperature, the more troops could be loaded. The pilots would calculate the amount of weight that we could carry. I would insure that they loaded the correct amount. Then again, in the case of an emergency, we were sometimes overloaded, but we would take everyone out. There was never a thought about who might need us. With each flight, we carried whatever was needed; food, water, ammo, more troops, as well as the evacuations of the dead and wounded.

No one ever thought about the number missions that had to be flown. We laughed because if this had been during World War Two, after twenty-five combat missions, we would be going home. It would not be that way this time. We never knew the names of the operations that we were flying support for. It was just one mission after another. Years later, I would learn some their names after I left the country.

The biggest thought on my mind at this point was that of how do you rate wearing the Combat Aircrew Wings? The wings glistened in the sunlight on the chest of many of the Marine shirts. Some Marines told me the silver wings had three gold stars on them and they represented being shot at on three different missions and you get your wings. Then I heard that you get your wings when you get your first Air Medal, after twenty combat missions. I counted the first three times that I was shot at and stopped counting after the fifth or sixth time. Trying to keep counting the number of times that I was being shot at seemed silly. The silver wings were very important and special to an enlisted man. They represent your ability to function as a team, under the pressure and stress of combat conditions. One morning, I was handed my sterling sliver combat wings. I was never formally awarded them, but I certainly earned my wings.

The original members of HMM-164 had spent their thirteen months in Vietnam and were now rotating back to the States. They had overcome many of the problems with bringing a new helicopter into combat for the first time. Their experiences of flying, maintenance, and working in combat were very valuable to the new flight crews and mechanics. We would try to uphold the reputation, along with the traditions of HMM-164, that they had established.

From all of those that followed in their footsteps

Thank You For A Job Well Done!

MEDEVAC STANDBY

We would have to stand a duty called Medical Evacuation Flights, which was to pickup and bring out the wounded. These flights were known as Medevac Standby. Any mission could turn into a MEDEVAC mission, but this duty was different. These missions were at a land base and the different squadrons would have this assignment on a rotating basis. This duty lasted for a twenty four hour period and in any type of weather. I would preflight the chopper. The pilot would do his preflight inspection and sign for it. I would button the chopper up. The pilots would go to the Ready Room, while my gunner, the Corpsman (Medic) and I stayed with the chopper.

We had four stretchers set up inside the cabin. We used them as our beds. Other choppers were going out on missions, but not us or whoever had the MEDEVAC Duty. Sandwiches, along with coffee were brought to us. We were parked away from the other aircraft and just stayed there. We talked, laughed and slept there, for the entire time. You could only go to the bathroom, when you had a relief. A full crew had to be at the chopper at all times.

The chopper was ready to go day or night. We would never talk about or even think about the mission that we were ready to do. We talked and joked about home, women, parties and everything else. We tried to emotional detach ourselves from the mission that we were prepared to launch on. The pilots waited in the Ready Room for the location of the mission. Sometimes, there would not be a mission during this 24 hour period. It is like being in an ambulance waiting for the call for help. You know the call is coming, but not knowing where you are going or what type of call it is going to be. In this case, you know that the bullets will be flying and they would need our help. The tension and stress levels were very high, but you couldn't worry about it. We learned to live with it, because we had a job to do.

Without warning, the alarm would go off. The adrenaline started pumping and rushing through my veins. I jumped into the cockpit and started the APP, even sometimes started the engines. The pilots were coming on a dead run. Minutes meant everything and there were none to lose, someone could be bleeding to death. I took my position as the pilots got into their seats. The pilot took off the rotor brake and the blades began turning. In seconds, we were airborne. The pilots knew where we were going, but they only told us that there were some wounded Marines out there and we were getting them. On some missions, while we were heading to the landing zone, Doc (the Medic) would hand me his M-79 Grenade Launcher and he would take over my right side machine gun. I said to him that he was supposed to be a noncombatant. He replied that he was going to be a live noncombatant. I laughed because I liked the way that he was thinking.

We headed into the zone to pick up the wounded. I would be at the cabin door, watching the ground coming up and clearing the chopper into the zone. The wounded were brought in the back ramp. Some were able to walk while others were carried. They placed on our stretchers and strapped in. We were off to Charlie Med or to the Hospital Ship. After getting back into the air, we helped Doc with the treatment of the wounded. The injuries were all types from bullets, to shrapnel, to burns, to broken bones. Real life traumas, like in a hospital emergency room, were right in front of you. Nothing can prepare you for seeing the wounds, missing limbs and death. We were trained to impose this same destruction on the enemy. There were no classes on how to handle the emotional effects, especially when it happens to our fellow Americans. We worked through the shock of seeing the results of war. There was always the blood and guts of human suffering and tears. We comforted and cared the wounded as best we could. Most of the casualties made it to the medical centers for the more intensive care, while some did not. We were their ambulance. The chopper would fly out, pick up the wounded and bring them back for treatment. We were just doing our job. The Corpsmen of the Marines and the Medics of the Army were the real heroes. On the ground and in the air, they worked very hard treating the wounded. They were performing what would have been considered to be medical miracles in previous wars and saved many lives.

Clearing zone — HMM-164 1968 Cruise Book

Some landing zones were quiet, while others were hot with the fighting was still going on. No matter how many times that you would stand this duty, the fear factor was there for that twenty four hour period. It was always nerve racking, but no one ever spoke about it. I guess that was because you never knew where you might be flying. You just knew that it was going to be hot. We would fly back to the base and refuel the chopper. The pilots would park it and go back to the Ready Room. We cleaned the interior of the chopper of the evidence of the mission. The crew then tried to relax, until the alarm sounded again for the next mission. We never talked about what we had just been through. The mission was placed into the back of our minds, because there was always another flight to take. We were not robots, but fellow Americans with our memories and feelings. The mental pressure was there. You cannot erase these sights and sounds from your mind. These are the memories that the crews would have to live with. Don't think about it, just do your job!

I guess these were the most rewarding missions of which we flew, because the wounded needed our help. The Marines on the ground needed us. They could be engaged in the heat of battle when the call was sent out. The Grunts knew that we were coming and would be there for them. There were no two missions that were the same. Everyone on the flight crew knew the tension was almost unbearable and it took its' toll on us. The satisfaction of saving a life, made these missions the most worthwhile. No one knows the exact number of lives of the wounded were saved during this war by our flights, but there were plenty. Through their pain, you could tell by the smiles on their faces that they were glad to see you. They had a sense of relief, just by their being onboard.

Those that were wounded would have to live with their injuries for the rest of their lives. There would be medical problems for them, both physical and mental. They had given their bodies and souls for this country and their fellow Marines. What more is there to give, except for your life? The people that earned a Purple Heart Medal for their injuries and those that served with them, care and understand about their plight. The people back home could never understand their pain.

CARRIER OPERATIONS

Word was being rumored around that we were going aboard an aircraft carrier. This time the rumor was true. This would be the first time that an entire squadron of CH-46 helicopters would be deployed aboard a carrier in Vietnam. Everything needed for the squadron to operate was packed, loaded and flown to the ship. We were going aboard the U.S.S. Princeton (LPH-5). This ship had fought during World War II and now was converted to a helicopter carrier. We left the dusty base at MMAF and flew out to sea. I had never even seen an actual combat ship before. There it was in the South China Sea. At first sight, it looked very small, but it got larger as we flew closer. The ship was gigantic, like a floating island. We flew abroad and landed on its long wooden flight deck. After we parked our choppers and tied them down, we were directed to our sleeping quarters. You could really get lost on this ship, but we learned our way around.

It is amazing how you can learn to appreciate the little things in life. We could finally sleep at night, with good hot food and hot showers. There was no air conditioning, but then again, you don't miss what you never had. The ocean breezes made up for it. These sailors had the real life, but we would never tell them. What a way to fight a war, cruising at sea. The Princeton had a salty crew. (This means they had been on station off of the coast of Vietnam for a long time and they knew what they were doing.) We continued our combat flight operations into Vietnam every day. We made some very good friends on that ship, especially among the flight deck crews.

One afternoon, I was on the hanger deck working on a chopper, when a sailor went running by. There were some military policemen chasing him. They yelled for someone to stop him. Well, when you are on an aircraft carrier and you are out at sea, where can you go? No one tried to stop the sailor. This sailor reached the fantail of the ship and he never stopped. He leaped over the railing and dove right into the South China Sea. One of the escort ships picked him up. We later learned he had mentally snapped and he was going home. No one knows how the pressures will effect someone. I knew that I couldn't swim back to the States, but then again, maybe he could.

We were making administrative runs into the bases at Marble Mountain, DaNang and Chu Lai. These flights were considered to be milk runs or non-hostile flights. Then again, you could get shot at on any flight. They might be to pick up the mail, bring in or out replacement personnel and spare parts. We knew these flights as beer runs. We also picked the beer. You could hide several cases of beer on the chopper, without them being seen. There was no booze on the ship, but we took care of that. The flight deck sailors loved us for it. One night, we took the CO2 fire extinguishers and used them to cool down the beer. We didn't have any ice. The chopper was parked on the flight deck with the back end hanging over of the edge of the ship. We drank the beer, laughed, joked and had a ball. We threw the empty beer cans out of the ramp of the chopper. We just knew that the cans were going into the sea, so no one checked. Well, they all landed on the catwalk, on the side of the ship. Needless to say, a Naval Officer found them and the beer runs were severely curtailed, but were never really stopped.

The vast majority of the sailors stationed in Vietnam were aboard combat and support ships. They only saw the coastline. It was very seldom they were ever shot at, only when they got too close to the shore. The ship would move further out to sea and out of the range of the enemy guns. One sailor wanted to show his family back home what Vietnam really looked like. He gave me his camera and I took it with me on a flight into Vietnam. I shot a roll of film and gave it back to him. Now, he could really tell some real war stories.

We would man our choppers by sitting in the pilot's seat, whenever the chopper had to be moved. This was to apply the brakes and parking brake, when necessary. We would ride up and down the elevators to the hanger deck and to the flight deck. You had to have faith in the flight deck crews, because you could look down right into the ocean and see it rushing by. I didn't wear my Mae West either. There was no room for error. We would fix the chopper and then it was right back on the flight deck for the next mission. Who said that Marines and Sailors didn't get along? We all worked together to get to get the job done. The choppers were moved by tractors or even by hand, when necessary. Parking spaces on either deck was precious. We would sit in the pilot's seat and press the blade folding button. The blades rotated and were locked in position. The six blades then folded along the side of the helicopter's body. This reduced the amount of space that the choppers took up and they could fit on the elevators. The choppers were chained down, so they couldn't move as the ship rocked and rolled, while we were sailing or in port. The ship was always moving. The choppers were moved from their parking space to the numbered spots on the flight deck. The rotor blades were unfolded and we were ready for flight.

You just couldn't help thinking about this ship and the action that it saw during World War II. The gun tubs held the anti aircraft guns were there, but the guns were taken out. Try standing at the fantail, watching the wake of the ship, smelling the salt air and try to get the sense of the many people that had served on this ship. We were riding in a ship that had been a part of history. I thought about the men that had served on this ship. We were riding the same elevators as the fighter planes and taking off of the same long wooden flight deck, as they did. The stretchers with the wounded were loaded onto bomb elevators and lower to sick bay from the flight deck for medical treatment. The bomb elevators were the same ones used to rearm the aircraft during World War Two. There was a lot of honor and pride that surrounded this ship, as it sailed through the calm waters of South China Sea. Now we were making our own history, combined with hers.

One admin flight came back to the ship, when the chopper lost an engine. It landed just short of the ship and was in the water. We all knew these things could happen. The chopper was floating, while we watched as the crew throwing out everything, trying to lighten the load. Out went the mailbags, machine guns and anything else, including the beer, but it did not work. They did not have the power to takeoff. The chopper was supposed to float for two hours in the water. This is what the book said. Well, when the blades were shut down, the chopper rolled slowly to the right and sank, immediately. The entire crew got out into the water. They were rescued very quickly. As we watched the chopper sink, I placed this fact in the back of my mind, in the water, it will roll to the right. So much for the book! I don't know who wrote it, but there were a lot of things in the book that just didn't work in combat. We had to learn these things the hard way.

One of our choppers had lost power and crash landed on top of the military post office in DaNang. Everyone was able to walk away from this crash. For some reason, our mail really got screwed up after that. Life was still good, an ocean cruise and beer. We were still flying every day and the mental pressures were still there. If I wasn't flying, my brothers were. Standing there on the flight deck, watching the choppers takeoff still brought about worrying, even if it was unconsciously. Enemy action or mechanical problems were always in the back of your mind, but this happened to other squadrons and other Marines, not to us.

We sailed through one hell of a storm in the South China Sea. The ship was pitching back and forth. I was walking on the hanger deck and I could see the ship moving. It was actually twisting. I didn't know it was supposed to do that. It was not like being on a small ship, but it was rocking and rolling. We had stored our choppers on the hanger deck, to protect them from the weather. They were tied down and couldn't move. When the storm cleared, it was back to work.

One morning, we went onto the flight deck and there was a submarine surfacing. We were all excited for spotting the submarine. The sailors thought that we were nuts. It came along the side of the carrier. They were exchanging movies. We did not know that the carrier had been escorted by a submarine. The submarine then slipped back beneath the waves. I guess they tell you things on a need to know basis. I guess that we didn't need to know about it.

The carrier could not leave the combat area to resupply itself. We would sail about ten miles off the coast. A tanker or a resupply ship would pull along side and lines were shot across between the ships. Ropes and then cables were strung. Next came the jet fuel hoses. This was called underway replenishment. The same was done for the ship's fuel along with cargo. There was no stopping. When they were finished with resupplying the ship, we would resume flight operations.

To show you a twist of fate, I was sitting on Spot One, which is at the front of the ship. I had a load of cargo and several passengers on board. Seated next to my gunner was a Chaplain. I told him it was a hot day and that this takeoff would be close. I asked him to say a few words for us. I was only kidding, but how soon the truth came out. The pilot lifted the chopper into the air and we headed out in front of the ship.

Suddenly, the chopper lost power on one of the engines. The helicopter began to drop like a rock. I watched the flight deck go by, along with the anchor of the ship, as we lost altitude. One of my Marine passengers jumped up to run. Without thinking, I grabbed him and pushed him back into his seat. I don't know where he thought that he was running to. There was no way the ship could stop or avoid hitting us. Emergency water landing procedures began running through my mind. We were along for the ride and there was nothing we could do. As we neared the water, the power to the engine came back on, as the rear wheels nearly hit the water and we began to slowly rise. The chopper gained altitude and the engines worked fine. I never did figure out what happened to that engine. I must say that I said, "Thank You to the Chaplain and my Mother". Those prayers were certainly answered. How many of my nine lives did I use up that day? I guess that I will never know.

SOUTH SEAS CRUISE

One morning, we looked out and Vietnam was gone. The carrier had left the combat zone and was heading for the Naval Base located at Subic Bay in the Philippines. We still worked on the choppers, but there was no flying. This gave us a chance to catch up on the maintenance and getting the squadron back up to full flying strength. Sailors and Marines were sunbathing on the flight deck. The sun was hot and the cool sea breeze made the sailing enjoyable. There was time for relaxation and we really needed it. After several days, we sailed into the harbor of Subic Bay. Across the bay, there was the biggest ship that I had ever seen. It was the U.S.S. Enterprise. This ship took up one whole side of the harbor. It was a nuclear powered aircraft carrier, with about 5,000 people on board. It was so big and made the Princeton look very small. It is wonder that it even floated. The tugboats docked our ship on the other side of the harbor.

We were going on liberty (Leave) into the city of Alongapo. After leaving the ship, the first thing that I did was to call home and my mother answered the phone. We exchanged the news and that I was all right. I told her that the call was costing a lot of money and she said shut up and that she was paying for it. How could I say anything? It was good hearing her voice. I later learned that the call costed $150.00 for 32 minutes, but she never told me.

After being in combat since December, it was time to party. I had to learn about this too. We went into town with all of the warnings. Don't go here. Don't go there. Never be alone. It sounded like Vietnam. Well, there were girls and bars, but we didn't carry any weapons. Well the first night, we went to a little bar not too far from the ship. The Filipino women were beautiful and sexy. Well this night we sat there and began drinking. The bartender was pretty and she made a drink called a Zombie. Now, I had it before but she made it with crushed ice and pineapple. It was delicious. I had six of them. I had a little high but I was fine, at least for the moment. I walked to the door, opened it and the air hit me, that was the last thing that I really remembered.

I staggered out to the street and grabbed onto a light pole. Another Marine took me to the ship. Somehow I made it there and walked up the gangplank. The Marine Officer was at the top. I had my hat on side ways, like a British Revolutionary War style hat and I gave him a British Salute and walked across the hanger bay. I should have headed for my bed, if I was smart, but who said that I was and I didn't. Well, there was the Officers entrance and an Officer checking them in. I staggered over to him and gave him the same salute. I asked him about a pilot and he said, "Marine, you're drunk" and I replied, "Yes Sir, I am," now tell me if a certain pilot had come aboard. He said, "No." I replied, "Thank you, Sir" and somehow made it to my sleeping quarters. Naturally my bunk was on the top. I crawled up the other bunks and rolled into my bunk. That is where I melted until the next day. I did suffer a little but the Zombies were great. We were there for several days, but no more getting drunk.

The women were something else. No matter which bar that you went into, the girls knew who you were with the night before. They had a better intelligence system than the United States. If our system were as good as theirs, we would have known where to find the Viet Cong. You would approach a girl and want to take her to a hotel. She would reply that last night you were with another girl and usually name her. She would then say, "You are butterfly". This meant that you go from flower to flower. After some talking the girl would leave with you, but it would cost you. There is nothing like the softness of the touch of a girl or the sweet smell of her perfume.

We knew that this paradise was not going to last. A fight broke out one night in a bar, between the sailors from the Enterprise and those from the Princeton. It really didn't take much to start a fight. They had called the Princeton a boat and to a sailor those are fighting words. We naturally helped our sailor friends from the Princeton. Lumps and bruises were received on both sides. The Princeton was heading back to the States for refitting. It was going to get air conditioning and other equipment. We had to say goodbye to all of our friends, but it was their turn to head home. They were a good crew and their experience would be missed.

The squadron transferred to the U.S.S. Tripoli, which was a Landing Platform Helicopter (LPH -10). This ship was smaller than the Princeton, had a round bottom and a white concrete flight deck. This new ship had just come from the States and was made especially for helicopters. Our squadron flew aboard. The vacation was over. It was time to go back to work and to the business at hand. We had more injuries in Subic Bay than what we had suffered in Vietnam. Fights and sex had taken their toll, but who was complaining. With some bandages and a few shots of Penicillin, we were fine.

We sailed to the island of Okinawa and the squadron flew into the Marine Air Facility at Fatima Air Base. World War II Marines also fought for this island, but it wasn't the same as Wake Island. This was a modern base and had cities that had been rebuilt. We checked our aircraft over and secured them. We went to the barracks and we set out for the town. Party time again. It seemed like each place that we went to there was another scam game to get your money. Well, we went down to the city of NaHa, and a little section known as B. C. Street. This is where the partying was being done, as well as the danger. After being drunk in Subic Bay, I had learned my lesson. At least I thought that I had. I went into a barber shop for a haircut and got the special. This included a massage and oral sex (blow job). I was young and this was beyond belief.

We walked into a bar and began drinking. We were there for hours. Well, I did it again. This time I was nowhere near the base. I was drunk and staggered out into the street and right in front of a cab. The passenger was Larry LeGrand, another Marine Crew Chief from the squadron. He pulled me into the cab. He was also drunk, but we rode to the base. The last thing he remembers was that we both staggered through the main gate. The next two Marines that came through the gate were the Commanding Officer and the Executive Officer of our squadron. They were stone cold sober and must have thought we were a total disgrace to the squadron. Somehow, we found our way back to our barracks. The guys said that we came through the doors, head to head and shoulder to shoulder. We walked down the middle of the squad bay stopped and fell into our bunks. Someone had taken our picture that night. We were voted the Number One Drunks in the Squadron for that night. We thought this was an honor because we certainly did try hard to earn it.

The next morning was like going through hell. We went to our aircraft first thing in the morning. There were no flights scheduled, but we had to preflight our choppers, well at least we were supposed to. I crawled up on the tunneling on top of the chopper and began to stagger on the small walkway. I grabbed onto one of the rotor blades to keep from falling and slid down to the side to stub wing. There was no way that I could checkout the chopper. I went into the cabin and pulled out a stretcher and set it up. I crawled onto it and went to sleep. My section leader woke me up and asked me if my chopper was okay and replied yes. I went back to sleep. I woke up at 4:30 in the afternoon and was still drunk. It is rough being the Number One Drunks. Everyone else was going on liberty, but Larry and I didn't. We slept that night away. There would be other nights to catch up on what we missed.

After surviving that wild night and a night of rest, it was time to do it again. We went to another bar that was on the second floor. As soon as you walked in, the women would come up to you and start asking for drinks. We were living for today, so the women sat down at our table. They ordered pink Champagne that later turned out to be ginger ale. We were drunk and they were sober, but they talked to us nicely and we ate it up. Hour after hour and talking, we all knew that we were going to be lucky and go home with a girl. As the evening went on and it was getting near closing time, we noticed that the women were going to the ladies room, but none were coming out. One of the guys went into the ladies' room and found that there was a door. The women were leaving by a side door and leaving us there. Well, a fight started with the bouncers and chairs were thrown, as well as bottles and glasses. Somebody yelled, M. P.'s. We all ran through the ladies' room, out the side door and onto the street. We made our way back to the base. We were all wearing civilian clothes, so no one knew where we had come from. So ended another wild night. I did learn the hard way and there were a few great nights on the island.

On one morning, I was working on my chopper on the flight line of the base. I looked up and saw a strange airplane flying over the base. I could usually recognize any aircraft and know what kind it was. This plane was different. It was black and looked like a long needle with a delta tail. I asked one of the guys stationed at the base, who had also seen this same plane, what kind of plane was it? He replied, "You did not see it." I replied, "Yes, I did see it". I received the same response. You didn't see it. This meant that the plane was a secret, but I did not know that then. It was another need to know basis, and I guess that I didn't need to know. For years, I would draw a picture of the plane that I had seen fly by and no one could tell me what airplane it was. I never forgot the plane and what it looked like. Years later, I learned that the airplane that I had seen flying over Okinawa in April of 1967 was the SR-71 Blackbird. Everyone, back in the world, knew of this super secret spy airplane, but I didn't see it. Who was I going to tell about it?

During this month, I was promoted to the rank of Corporal, which means a lot to an enlisted Marine. At this rank, you get the red stripe on your dress blue uniform pants. You are now a Non-Commissioned Officer. It is almost like graduating all over again. Gone were the days of spit shined shoes, starched uniforms and dress parades. Well, there were no dress blues in Vietnam and no parades or formal ceremonies that this uniform could be worn. I would have to just wait to get back to the States to wear my dress blue uniform.

THE BATTLE OF THE HILLS

This was April 1967, we were really young, really dumb. We were the best and we knew it. The squadron flew back aboard the carrier and we picked up the infantry, Second Battalion Third Marines (pronounced two three — 2/3), the Grunts. They are the ones that actually take and occupy ground from the enemy. The U.S.S. Tripoli was ready for anything, as we headed out to sea. The word was that we were heading to Taiwan, for some more fun and games, well this rumor wasn't true. There was a problem in Vietnam and we were the Special Landing Force (S.L.F.). We were the emergency force that would respond when there was trouble.

There were two special landing forces stationed aboard carriers off the coast of Vietnam. Each force had a battalion of Marines and a helicopter squadron. They were known as S.L.F. Alpha and Bravo. We were S. L. F. Bravo and arrived back off of the coast of Vietnam. We were heading for the base at Khe Sanh. This Marine Battalion was armed with the new M-16 rifle and would be the first unit to use it in combat. The rifle was black and plastic that made it look like a toy, a Matty Mattel Toy. The Marines fired the rifles off of the ship and they worked fine. We readied our choppers and were scheduled for a morning launch. The Marines of 2/3 were going to war.

We sat on the flight deck of the carrier with our engines running and rotor blades turning. Out came the Marines, carrying their equipment on their backs. Fifteen at a time made their way to the choppers. We loaded them up. The first wave of choppers took off. The second wave of choppers was brought out, spotted on the flight deck and loaded. The flight after flight took off and headed out over the South China Sea. The troops sat there, with no outwards signs of nervousness. They laughed and joked with each other. From being aboard the ship, we got to know some of them and they were not only Marines, but our friends. Upon arriving at the base, we dropped them off at the staging area. It was off again and back to the ship for another load of troops and cargo. The battalion had arrived and was ready for action.

It was the Battle of the Hills or the First Battle of Khe Sanh, as it would be later called. The Battles of Hill 881 North, Hill 881 South, and Hill 861 were the hills that were around and overlooking the air base at Khe Sanh. The enemy had been located and the fighting began. I guess that this was the first time that I realized exactly who we were actually fighting. The newspapers and news programs always talked about the Viet Cong or the V. C. They were a rag tag outfit of untrained civilians waging a guerilla war in South Vietnam. Well, there might have been some, but we were engaged with North Vietnamese Regular Army (NVA). They had been fighting for years and were good. They were as good as any Army in the world, but they were all just Charlie to us.

The Marines of 2/3 with the new M-16 rifle engaged the enemy, but they had a problem. Things started going wrong. The rifles began jamming. This is the last thing that you want to happen in combat. The rifles would fire one bullet and wouldn't eject the bullet casing to fire the next bullet, causing it to jam. The Marines were trying to clear the weapons, so they would shoot again. They were being killed and wounded, because of this malfunction of the rifle. The call went out for MEDEVACS. This call meant only one thing. The Marines needed us.

Over and over, we flew into countless landing zones with the battles raging. Time on the ground was very limited. The longer that we were on the ground, the greater the chance of Charlie zeroing in on us and hitting the chopper. The grunts knew that we were coming and would pop a colored smoke grenade to pinpoint their location. We would swoop in low and fast over the tree line to touch down in the L Z. We worked throughout the days and nights, picking up the wounded, dying and dead Marines. These flights were transporting the casualties to the first aid station at Khe Sanh or taking them to Charlie Med. Some of the wounded were brought back to the Tripoli. Many others of the more seriously wounded were carried to the U.S.S. Repose or Sanctuary; the two hospital ships that were stationed off the coast of Vietnam. They were painted white with big red cross markings on the sides. These ships had the best medical facilities and doctors that this country had to offer. There was a helicopter landing pad located at the rear of these ships. We would fly aboard and drop off the wounded. It was back into the air and the return flight back to Khe Sanh and another mission.

There was a Marine on a flight with me that asked me for my M-14 rifle to take with him into the field. I couldn't let him take my rifle. Besides, it took a different size bullet. The Marines were carrying a ramrod with them. If their rifle jammed, they would use the ramrod to knock the empty shell casing out of the chamber. What a hell of a way to fight a war, it was like being in the Revolutionary War, with a flintlock rifle. One shot and that was it. There was a sense of fear in his eyes as he left my chopper. He did not have any faith in his weapon. Your weapon is your life. It might be the only thing between life and your death. Whether he made it or not, I really don't know. I never saw him again, but I hope that he did survive.

Some people back in the States tried to blame the Marines for not maintaining the rifle correctly. It was said that the rifle had to be kept clean to fire properly. Well tell me, how do you crawl up the sides of mountains through the mud, dirt, and water and still keep the rifle clean? This was not the problem, but a faulty extractor on the bolt that caused the problem or the wrong type of gunpowder in the bullets. Either way the blame goes all the way back to the manufacturer and the military, but not Marines that had to use it. No one will ever know exactly how many Marines died because of this rifle, but there were many. After that, I never had any faith in that rifle, no matter how many improvements they made to it. Too many Marines were wounded and died behind that piece of faulty equipment. We believed we were using the best equipment. Well that was proven to be wrong in combat, with the blood and lives of Marines that had to use it.

At the end of the day, we would fly back to a base camp or to the ship. Even then, we didn't know if there might be an emergency resupply or Medevac mission. The pilots went for their debriefings of the missions and to get some rest. The Crew Chief and mechanics began working on the choppers and doing the necessary maintenance to keep them flying. A chopper is not like a car or truck. If something goes wrong, there was no pulling over to the curb to fix it. There was no bailing out. Anything that went seriously wrong could kill you and the entire crew. Everything has to be working right before you leave the ground. Our rest came when the maintenance was completed and the choppers were ready for the next flight.

BREAKER PATROL

We continued to fly both day and night missions in support of the Marines battling for the Hills. Over and over, we flew in all types of weather. We were flying into the face of death on a daily basis and had been very lucky. Several people had been hurt due to crashes and accidents, but nothing serious. May 10, 1967 came and our luck ran out. I was aboard the carrier and on the flight deck. We were scheduled for a morning launch to Khe Sanh. The word was received that during the night, Captain Paul Looney had been killed. Once again it was a wake up call and a **REALITY CHECK**, you could get killed doing this job. He had come to Vietnam with HMM-262 and transferred to HMM-164 at the same time that I did. He was one of the best pilots in the squadron and was flying with one of the best crews. How could this happen? This thought had run through my mind, as I was preparing my aircraft for my mission.

We mounted our machine guns. I put on my Mae West and bullet bouncer. The pilots got onboard and we took off. It was a two-chopper flight heading toward Vietnam. As we crossed over the beach, the pilot radioed the ship and reported, "Feet Dry," meaning that we were over the land. We headed inland and flew up the valley to the base at Khe Sanh, being followed by our wingman. All of this time, my heart is pounding, not knowing what we were heading for. It was a very quiet flight. There was no laughing or joking as in normal flights. I guess the entire crew was thinking about the loss of one of our own.

Upon landing at the base, we walked over to the chopper that was piloted by Capt. Looney. The CH-46 was all shot up. It looked like Swiss cheese. There were bullet holes all up and down the chopper. Inside there was very little blood. We learned the story behind the mission. There was a Marine Recon patrol that had run into trouble. It was a night mission.

They had run into a meat grinder and needed an immediate extraction. The flight of two 46's and two Huey gun ships took off. As the choppers approached the L Z, the NVA gunners opened up. Although the gun ships escorted them into the area, they could not fire, because the enemy was too close to our troops. The NVA gunners had wounded everyone, as their bullets ripped through the thin skin on the first chopper. His wingman also took some hits. They had to abort the landing because of the heavy volume of enemy fire. Both choppers returned to the base at Khe Sanh.

Two more of our choppers were dispatched for the emergency extraction. Capt. Looney was piloting the lead chopper and he located the patrol. Being at night, there is no way of hiding a big helicopter. They needed illumination to land. Flares were dropped to light up the area. The enemy knows where you are going and that makes you a sitting duck. He made his first approach and the enemy guns started firing. He aborted the landing. He made his second approach along the valley. The patrol was on a small mesa at the end of the valley. The chopper reached the end of the valley and Capt. Looney flew up the side of the hill and landed. The chopper was too far away from the Marines. He had missed the patrol and had to come around again to get them. As he came around for the third time, the enemy opened up again. This time the bullets found their mark. Capt. Looney was hit and he got out of the cockpit. The copilot was then hit in the foot, but was able to fly the chopper back to the base. The landing zone was too hot for a chopper to land, so the Marines were left there. The chopper had taken a lot of hits by bullets and had more than 150 holes in it, but it kept on flying. Everyone had been medevaced for treatment. Capt. Looney would later die of his wounds. It was a very bad scene.

Now it was morning and the Marines were still out there. A sister squadron was ready to get the Marines out (I think that they were from HMM-265 or 165), and they took off. I knew that they would get them out. I refueled my chopper and got ready for the day's work. My pilots were at the ready room, while my gunner and I were at my chopper. Our thoughts were for our squadron members that had been hurt and looking at their shot up chopper. After several minutes, there was the sound of the choppers coming back. As they were landing, I could see the red hydraulic fluid pouring out of one of the choppers and down its side. It looked like the chopper was bleeding. It had taken nine hits and one bullet had struck a hydraulic line. They had to abort the rescue attempt. I spoke to the Crew Chief and was told that the zone was hotter than Hell. He said that he had shot one V. C. with his pistol, because the machine gun would not swing down far enough to use it. They didn't even get on the ground, before taking fire. Luckily, no one onboard his chopper was hurt. It was definitely a meat grinder — flying into Hell.

There were still three Marines out there. My pilot came, looked at me and said, "We're next!" All kinds of red lights began going off in my head. I asked my pilots about what kind of support were we going to have. He said that we would have two Phantoms (F-4's) jets and two Huey Gun Ships. I told him that was the same thing that the other choppers had and it didn't do any good. I then told him that I wasn't going. Flying was a voluntary assignment and you could quit flying at any time. This sounded like a good time to quit. My pilot looked at me strangely. He told me to think about my decision. The pilots left me for the briefing on the mission. My mind was racing and I was really afraid. You can get scared and nervous during mortar and rocket attacks, a strike mission or even a medevac mission, but this was different. I was going to be the target. My chopper would take the lead and would be going in first, with my crew. We would be some big, slow-moving targets, just like the other choppers. The enemy was waiting for us. The odds were stacked and they were not in my favor.

No one ever knew about the reoccurring dream that I was having. I had dreamed many times about my lying on a floor and holding my stomach. I didn't know if I had been stabbed or shot. I had been wounded, but I knew that I was dying. I knew this mission was going to bring this dream true. I was to die on this mission. I thought that I was going to be a dead man, and broke out in a cold sweat, almost shaking. I thought for a moment and then caught my breath. If we had just left and did the mission, I think that it would have been different, but there was too much time for thinking.

We had been taught to react to a situation. Here I was sitting there, just thinking. My mind was taking over and thinking about what could happen. Looking at the shot up choppers and thinking about the injured crews didn't help either. Fear was taking over and this is what was waiting for me and my crew. There is a difference between being scared and being afraid. I don't know what happened, but I guess that it was when my training kicked in or was it my Esprit De Corp to the Marines or was it my responsibility to my crew? I really can't say exactly what it was, but I knew that I had a job to do. Those Marines needed my chopper and me. I was a member of a helicopter crew and this was my job. I cleared my head and the thoughts of the dream left from my mind.

I turned to my gunner and told him to get all the ammo from the other shot up choppers. I went over to the ammo shed and got four rifles, ammo and several kinds of grenades. We loaded my chopper up. We linked several boxes of .50 cal. ammo together, so that we would not have to reload flying into the zone. My pilot returned and I told him that we were ready to go. He looked at me and smiled. He took one look at the inside my chopper and said, "What is this?" The chopper was filled with bullets, grenades and rifles. I told him if we were going down, it was going to be in a blaze of glory. He just shook his head and got into the cockpit, along with the copilot. We took off along with our wingman following. There was no briefing, but we knew what we had to do. There were still three Marines out there and the V. C. was using them as a helicopter trap. They knew we were not going to leave them out there and that we were coming back. This time, it was my turn.

The flight was quiet as we headed for the mountains and the three Marines. It really didn't take us long to get to the area. The sky was clear with bright sunlight with a few clouds. There was no hiding or sneaking up on them. The enemy could see us coming and knew exactly where we were going. I was listening to the radio through the ICS and my pilot talking to the guys on the ground. It was about 10 A.M., they had been awake all night, fighting for their lives and all were wounded. We circled a few miles from the landing zone. I watched the jets make their runs and bomb the area. The Huey gun ships strafed and rocketed the mesa. This was Marine Close Air Support at its best. This was the same thing that had been done earlier. It all looked so deadly and totally devastating. The smoke cleared. This firepower could not be used at night, because of the fear of hitting our own troops. With the sunlight, pilots could place their ordinances exactly where it was needed.

There was a clearing in the middle of the mesa with several bomb craters in it. My pilot asked me if we were ready and I replied, "Ready, you're making me late for lunch, lets go." When you get scared or nervous, you can say some silly things. There was no fear at this time, only the mission at hand and to complete. Our wingman would stay high, in the event we were shot down and needed to be rescued. We headed for the L Z. My gunner and I took our positions on our machine guns. We had a job to do and now it was our turn.

We banked to the right and headed for the zone. My chopper began to slow down, as we neared the L Z. We were trying to locate the Marines. We were about 50 feet off of the ground and the tree lines opened up, looking like flash bulbs going off at a cameramen's convention, from the muzzle flashes of the enemy rifles being fired at us. We were a very big target, as we approached the landing zone. We pressed our triggers firing back. We were shooting 20 to 50 round bursts. The chopper vibrated from the recoil of the machine guns. The pilot began yelling over the ICS, for us to shoot in short bursts. There was no time to respond to him. He didn't know we had linked the boxes of ammunition together. With the wind traveling about a hundred miles an hour over the barrel, the gun barrels were not going to overheat. Our bullets were cutting down trees.

I spotted the three Marines huddled in a bomb crater, in the middle of a clearing and told the pilots. Knowing exactly where they were was extremely important, so we could land as close to them as possible. We passed over the landing zone, gaining speed and reaching for more altitude, as we pulled back into the sky. The Marine on the radio went crazy. He was begging us to pick them up, in no uncertain terms. I never thought about the dangers or even the bullets being fired at us. I was busy doing my job as a part of my flight crew, trying to suppress the enemy fire.

We circled again and turned back for the zone. At this point, I heard another pilot's voice on the radio. This pilot called to the Marines on the ground. He said, "I am a Huey Slick. This means that I don't have any guns. I am going to be on the ground for five seconds, all I want to see is three assholes moving." There was a pause and the Marine on the ground rogered the radio call.

As we came around for our second pass at the landing zone, the Huey Slick followed us. This Huey chopper was a much smaller target. We came along the tree line. We began firing, while the Huey broke for the zone. We circled the zone, and continued firing. The Huey came in low, fast and slid to a stop in the L Z., near their target. I saw the three wounded Marines start running for the chopper. We continued to eat up real estate with our .50 caliber machine guns. You could have called us lumberjacks, because you could see the trees falling apart from the bullets. We made a tight circle around the clearing, while the Huey was on the ground.

You would have thought that those three Marines were running in the Olympics and doing a hundred yard dash. I watched them running for the chopper, while still firing at the enemy. You would have never thought that they all were wounded. They had been up all night fighting for their lives. It was one, two, three, and they were in the chopper. The Huey lifted off and made its way down the valley. We then broke away from the area. The Phantom Jets then came in and really bombed the area. I never met or saw those three Marines again, not to mention the Huey crew that had made the rescue. We cleared the area and headed back to Ky Sanh.

The mission was well worth it. We had saved three fellow Marines. We were not heroes, just Marines doing our job. The mission was finished. It would be years later, I learned that there had been seven Marines out there and that the other four bodies were never recovered. Everyone had received awards. There were Purple Hearts, Air Medals, Silver Stars, and the Navy and Distinguish Flying Crosses handed out. Needless the say, we got nothing, but one combat mission. There was no glory, we just did our job. It had been a very costly mission: four helicopters had been shot up, several crewmembers had been wounded, one pilot was killed and four Grunts that would never come home. They were all Marines. Some more prayers were answered. It would be thirty years later before I would learn the name of this mission, it was "Breaker Patrol."

This mission was over. We flew back to the base at Khe Sahn and continued with resupply missions for the rest of the day. We then flew back to the ship at the end of the day. It was good to be there. The thoughts that had been going through my mind about the dream were gone. I had flown into Hell and had come back. How many times can you cheat death and come out a winner? The enemy, mechanical failure, adverse weather conditions or human error, all could have brought about death or serious injury to the flight crew. The fear really didn't resurface until I thought about what had happened. By this time it was over. Fear can be a disabling force. There is nothing wrong with being scared. It is natural. It is what you do with fear that is what's important. I had flown on many missions, but the thought of fear never arose. I overcame my fears on this mission.

You are here for this moment and gone the next. The loss of our fellow Marines still hurt. There was no time to be thinking of what had happened to them. The battle for the hills surrounding Khe Sahn continued. There were many more bloody engagements to follow until the Marines finally won the battle, but we paid a heavy price for those hills. The enemy paid an even higher price for tangling with the Marines.

Was there a feeling of revenge? I don't think there was. There was the sense of the loss of a brother that you never get use too. Can you find the person that fired the fatal shots? I doubt it. Had the bullets, bombs and rockets killed the enemy? We don't really know that either. We hoped so. This was war and men died on both sides.

There was no way to bring our Marines back to life. After the mission was over, there was plenty of time for thinking and for feeling. There is a certain degree of numbness that comes over you, when it comes to the death of a squadron mate. We held our memorial service for him. We still couldn't dwell on it and no time for grieving. There was always another job to do, another flight to take and another mission. Others were depending on us. I never saw Captain Looney again. He was gone and his body was shipped home for burial. He was like my neighbor being from Massachusetts, married, and the father of a little girl, who would never know him.

Special Note:

In May 2003, the remains of the four missing Marines of Breaker Patrol were located and later identified by the Joint POW/MIA Accounting Command.

Lance Corporal Samuel A. Sharp — was interned on April 5, 2005 in San Jose, California.

Remains of L/Cpl Sharp — Second Lieutenant Heinz Ahlmeyer — Sergeant James N. Tycz — Navy Corpsman HM3 Malcolm T. Miller were interned at Arlington National Cemetery in Washington, D.C. on May 10, 2005. Thirty eight years to the day of their deaths.

May They Rest In Peace

Survivors of the patrol that were rescued are:

Lance Corporal Clarence R. Carlson — Private First Class Carl Friery — PFC Steven D. Lopez

BREAKER PATROL HAS RETURNED HOME — WELCOME HOME MARINES MISSION COMPLETED

COMBAT MISSIONS

The flight crews were not assigned to the same chopper all of the time. Only the Crew Chief stayed with the same helicopter. It was a constant blending of different pilots and gunner, along with their personalities. It was the luck of the draw as to what pilots, gunners and missions that were assigned to my aircraft. No matter who was onboard the chopper, we all knew our jobs and had to function as a team.

With each flight, we saw more of the countryside than what the vast majority of the people in Vietnam had ever seen. There were very few large cities and they were mainly along the coast. The majority of the I Corp region was sparsely populated. The hills were covered with thick green foliage. We would fly over fishing villages, along with small rural villages. We flew over the rice paddies, small farms, as well as the rivers with their arrow shaped fishing traps. Most of the Vietnamese people did not have the simple pleasures of life like clean running water, plumbing, or even electricity. We, as Americans have taken these things for granted. The visible signs of the war, bomb and shell craters that scarred the landscape, were all around.

As for the South Vietnamese people, did they want us there in their homeland? Did they really care why we were there? Why were we the ones sent to this far off land? We fought for our own survival. If survival included the South Vietnamese people, all well and good. They worked in their rice paddies, farmed, fished and cared for their families as best that they could. This was the land of bicycles, motor scooters, and water buffaloes, not to mention the pretty women. The regular civilian didn't have anything to say about the war. Generation after generation knew only fighting, killing and dying. It was a way of life for them. They all were just pawns in this game of chess, the victims of war. Someone was always fighting over their land. During World War Two, it was the Japanese, then it was the French and now it was the North Vietnamese. More than thirty years of conflict had raged throughout this land. They were just caught up in the politics of four or five countries: North Vietnam, South Vietnam, Russia, China and the United States.

We carried South Vietnamese Soldiers, the Army of the Republic of Vietnam, known as ARVNS. The problem with carrying them was that we did not speak their language and we did not know who they were. Were they loyal to South Vietnam or were they actually Viet Cong or North Vietnamese sympathizers? We knew there were infiltrators in their Army, did we have any on board? Some would smile at you. Maybe they were glad to be onboard the chopper. Other soldiers would just stare at you. Were they afraid of flying or were they just waiting for a chance to shoot you? You never knew who the enemy was or where they were. There were stories of Vietnamese soldiers leaving live grenades in the choppers when they left. After the chopper took off, the grenade would explode. As soon as the Vietnamese soldiers got out, we would check the inside the chopper for anything that didn't belong there. We always kept one eye on them and one hand on our pistol. I think they could also feel the distrust that we had for them. Even after carrying our own troops, we would check the cabin area, just in case something was dropped. Accidents do happen, but you can't afford one in the air. It is a long way down to the ground.

The squadron was flying some missions that we were putting out Marine Recon Teams, all around the Khe Sanh area. They were four and five man teams. They were checking the areas for enemy troop movements. In the middle of the afternoon, there was a call over the radio from one of the teams that we had placed in the field. They had walked into more than what they could handle. They needed an immediate extraction. My pilot without hesitation turned the chopper around and headed for the area of the embattled team. This was near the

Laotian border. The team popped a colored smoke grenade, so we could locate them. We turned and began to start a spiral. The chopper was going down. There were hills all around, as we began flying through a valley toward the L Z.

We were a big tempting target. With each landing, we could be flying into an enemy ambush. The enemy did not have to be close to our troops to fire at us. Bullets, rockets and missiles can travel great distances to reach their target. Everyone down on the ground could see and hear us approaching. Without any warning, I began to hear the sounds of pop, pop, pop. Someone was shooting. I looked out of my window and didn't see anything. I did not know exactly where our troops were, so I couldn't shoot without seeing my target. We didn't want to hit our own troops. I turned and looked out the port side of the chopper. The entire side of the hill was flashing with muzzle flashes. It looked like another cameramen's convention. These were not our troops, but the enemy and they were shooting at us. My gunner, a Gunnery Sergeant was on his machine gun looking out. He was bent over, just staring out of the window. He had frozen on the gun. Without thinking I kicked him, dead in the butt, with my steel toed boot. He began shooting his gun and firing bullets at the enemy.

We flew in fast and low over the trees, as the chopper landed in the zone. Our protection was two Huey gunships. They flew in and fired machine gun bullets and rockets at the mountain side, to suppress the enemy fire. The Recon team ran onboard. There were a couple of the Marines that were wounded. We got them all out. We lifted up and flew out through the valley. My chopper had survived flying through a hail of bullets. We treated the wounded on the flight back to the base. After dropping the team off, I checked the chopper over. There was not one hit in it.

My gunner turned to me and said that he was going to bring charges against me for striking a Staff NCO. He outranked me, but I was the Crew Chief and in charge, while we were on the chopper. Now we were back on the ground and he was throwing his weight at me. I responded to him that if he wrote me up, I would inform everyone he had froze on the gun. No one would fly with someone that is afraid to fight. Well, he didn't write me up. I was a Corporal and remained the same until the day I got out of the Marines. I guess that he might have found another way of getting back at me. Thanks Mom for the prayers.

The helicopter was a great tool, but there were many long hours of inspections and maintenance to be done to keep them in the air. Our pilots were some of the best. The pilots had their own things to worry about like the matter of flying this big chopper and putting it into areas that were not long, flat concrete runways. They watched the gauges, adjusting the power and maintaining control of this complex machine, as well as the communications and navigation. Some L Z's were as big as a postage stamp. I would guide us in and out of the zones, watching for any obstacles and where the rear wheels were touching down. Once the chopper was safely on the ground, my attention turned to the loading or unloading of passengers and cargo. Then it was back into the air and the next mission. There was a lot to be done and the flight crew was very busy.

Sitting in Crew Chief Seat with helmet on.

We flew a mission to pick up a recon team from the side of a mountain. There was no place to land and we could not use the cable hoist. The pilot backed the chopper into the side of the mountain and held it in a steady hover. They were sitting there in their armor plated seats staring out into nothing but sky and watching their gauges. We were like a sitting duck and my pilots must have been sweating nervously. I went to work going to the rear of the chopper to the ramp and let it down. I put on my gunner's belt and clipped it to a cargo ring to anchor myself in. Reaching out of the back ramp, I pulled the men aboard, one by one. As the last man was pulled into the chopper, my pilot called for me over the ICS to come into the cockpit. I closed the ramp and ran up front to the cockpit, there had to be something wrong.

The pilot pointed to the engine gauges. We had one engine running at 60% power, while the other engine was running at 110%. The two engines were supposed to be matched at 100% of its power. The pilot was afraid that we did not have enough power to lift off. I understood his concerns, but this did not make any sense to me. We were not on the ground, but still hovering on the side of the mountain. I had to troubleshoot the chopper to figure out the problem. The other engine gauges were reading okay. I ran to the rear and opened the engine access doors to check the engine actuators. They were fine and in their proper positions. The jet engine exhaust temperatures were normal. The engine was not made to run at 110% for long and would burn itself up. I then went back to the cockpit and got in between the pilots. I said that we should have enough power. I thought for a moment and said that we should head down the side of the mountain. By the time that we reached the floor of the valley, we should have enough air speed to pull out.

Without saying another word, the pilot lifted the chopper up and banked it to the right. We cleared the trees and headed for the floor of the valley. The helicopter was racing down the side of the mountain just above the treetops, while picking up speed. The engines' power matched up at 100%. We pulled up and headed for the safety of the sky. As we gained altitude, the pilot looked at me and he was smiling. I looked at him like he was crazy. He laughed and told me that I was right. He actually listened to me. It sounded right to relieve the load on the engines and they would match up their power. I only knew all about the chopper and how to fix it, but they flew them. What did I know about flying it? If I was wrong, we would have certainly crashed and burned. We would have made a very big dent in Vietnam. We flew the team back to their base. I checked the engines and gauges and found that there was nothing wrong with them. The engines did not have any damage and worked fine. Another mission was completed and another prayer answered.

MORE MISSIONS

The most dangerous missions were those where we couldn't land and had to make a cable hoist pick up. While en route to the L.Z, I would rig the cable and open the "Hellhole". The Hellhole was a trap door in the middle of the cabin on the floor. When the two panels were open and you stepped in there, it was one step to Hell. There were no parachutes on board. We would locate the person to be picked up and the pilot would bring the chopper into a hover. Now, talk about a sitting duck. The pilot had to hold the chopper steady and in place. I lowered the cable with the rescue collar, or later a jungle penetrator, that brought the person up into the chopper. It was a long slow process. I never really thought about the fear or the time it took. I was too busy doing my job. Now once the danger was over, the thoughts of what could have happened raced through my mind. You had to learn to deal with the fear and stress. If not, you would go crazy. The sights, sounds, and smells of war will stay with you for a lifetime.

Any night flight mission brought about its own fears, namely not being able to see anything. It would be an emergency Medevac or emergency resupply mission of ammunition. There would be at least two 46's and two Huey gunships for protection. We would take our position on our guns and stare into the black void of the night, trying to see the landscape. The pilots were directed to the position of the troops. We would turn off our running lights and head for the L Z; this would hide us from the enemy as long as possible, until we neared the ground. We watched for the signal from the troops on the ground for our landing spot. Out of the darkness, we appeared over the zone. The pilot would turn on the spotlight, but not for long, while we landed. The red cabin lights were turned on, while we guarded the ramp to insure that our troops were coming onboard. There were stories of the enemy rushing the rear of the chopper and shooting at the crew. We would drop off the supplies or pick up the wounded. We would not be on the ground very long and it was back into the air.

The Army had Huey Slicks for MEDEVAC missions. They had red crosses on them and were unarmed. These were known as Dust Off Missions for them. They had Hueys' that transported troops and cargo, along with CH-47's and Sky Cranes for hauling heavy loads. The Marine Corps was not so lucky as to have so many special helicopters for special missions. We had to do it all. We did medevac, Search and Rescue for downed pilots, along with Aircraft Drone recovery. We did resupply (internal and external loads) missions, troop transporting, Recon transports and any other mission that could be thought of. The CH-46 also did aircraft retrieval. We flew our own slicks. They were choppers without armor plating, and without a rear ramp, to make them as light as possible. We would pick up other choppers and aircraft that were downed in the field. This job was done by the CH-37 and then the 46, until the bigger CH-53 arrived In-Country.

We would also carry external cargo loads that were slung beneath the chopper. The Crew Chief would lie on the floor behind the Hellhole and watch the load. The big cargo hook had an emergency release switch. If something happened to the load or it began to oscillate for some reason that could endanger the safety of the helicopter, it could be dropped by either the pilot or the Crew Chief. I would direct the pilot as to picking up the load and to where to set the load down. The pilots sat up front and could not see the load.

The squadron also flew flights called Shining Brass or Special Operations Group (SOG) missions. These were missions carrying Special Forces and Chinese Mercenaries over the border into Laos on SOG Missions. The Special Forces (The Green Berets) were an elite section of the Army. They were great as a unit, but there were only ten or fifteen that accompanied the Chinese. They would observe enemy movement and also ambush them. Sometimes they would run into more than what they could handle and would need an immediate helicopter extraction. Most of these missions were secret and are still considered to be classified. We weren't there, enough said.

Sometimes, the mission was to bring out the dead. Emotionally, these were the toughest missions. Flying back to the base or ship with the bodies of Marines or soldiers is not pleasant by any means. The bodies would be loaded, sometimes like stacking wood. Most were in body bags or ponchos, while others weren't. We didn't know who they were, but we knew what was in the bags. They were the bodies of our fellow Marines. These Marines would not grow any older. There is really a lot of truth in the saying, "War Is Hell." There were too many of these flights.

On one flight, we flew into an L Z with three body bags for three that were killed in action. I handed the bags to a Marine. He only took one body bag. He walked over to a hole and took out his bayonet. He stabbed something three times and placed the items into the one body bag and zipped it closed. He walked back to me and handed me the bag. I shouted to him over the noise of the chopper, that there was supposed to be three bodies. He said, "There they are!" During the night, a mortar round had landed in their fox hole and exploded. He said that this was all that was left of them. Talk about reality. Here I was holding the remains of three grown men in one hand. The bag weighed about twenty pounds. Who were they? Where were they from? They never knew what happened or what hit them. I knew what their families were going to be put through and their feelings because of Norman's funeral. There was really nothing left of these three Marines. They had lived and they had died together, but there would be three separate closed casket funerals back in the States.

This was war, trading lives for real estate and taking ground from the enemy. Our troops died from the enemy, they died from our own troops (good old friendly fire). I, personally don't think any fire that is coming at you is friendly fire, no matter who was firing it, and also they died from equipment that was defective. There were mistakes made, many of them; the wrong coordinates given, artillery rounds landing short, wrong markers, even troops being out of position. Nobody is perfect and there are mistakes that were made in every war. There were enough mistakes made in this one. You just prayed that you did not make a mistake that might cost an American his life.

The battles continued and we continued to do our job. We flew day in and day out, mission after mission, flight after flight. We fought to protect our brothers in arms and to get back to the States. We had been placed in this country and we had a year to do there. There were no battle lines and the enemy could be anywhere. Our friends were being wounded and killed. We were not the Generals or the policy makers, but our job was the dirty one. We did the job that we were trained to do. This was the real meaning of being a Marine - to fight our country's battles. Too many died doing their job.

Life was tough through the months of April and May 1967. The shiny appearance of being cocky had been worn off. We had been well seasoned by combat and we were now a salty squadron. Everyone knew their jobs and we gained the reputation of going anywhere that we were needed and at anytime. There were many, many long hours of flying and maintenance. I think back now, where was there any time for sleep? We were still aboard the carrier and when it was time to go to bed, sleeping was easy. There was even air conditioning on this ship. The Marines had won their battles around Khe Sanh, even with the problems with their rifles. Our squadron had received the Navy Unit Commendation for our support of the Battle of the Hills. We had a certain pride in our accomplishments and very proud of our unit. This battle had been very costly, both physically and emotionally. We were tired and could have used a rest. There was no rest, just another flight to take.

This was not like the Army. If there was something wrong with their chopper, the Crew Chief would tell the maintenance personnel and they would fix it. In the Marines Corps, we did not have the luxury of having so many people. The Crew Chief was also the mechanic. When there was maintenance to be performed, it was done by the Crew Chief. The policy in our squadron was that if your chopper wasn't flyable then you didn't fly either. There were times that we could take someone else's chopper on a mission, but that was few and far between. Every chopper was needed and the work went on continuously to make them flyable. Flying was the easy part.

For the month of June 1967, our squadron had totaled the most flight hours of any other CH-46 helicopter squadron in Vietnam. My chopper had the most flight hours in our squadron for that month. I was then told that I was being grounded because my chopper was dirty. What time did I have to clean it? If I wasn't flying, then I would have had plenty of time to clean it. Sure my chopper was dirty and I was tired. I could have used a day off from flying just for the rest. I washed the chopper inside and out. I cleaned and shined it up. Using a combination of jet fuel and hydraulic fluid made my chopper shine. My chopper sat there with its green paint that was sparkling in the sunshine. It looked like a picture on a postcard. I was put back on flight status and my chopper was ready. I was off again on my first flight. The first landing zone that we went into was a sandy one. The sand was blown all over the chopper. The sandy grit stuck to the clean painted surfaces and it was dirty again. This was like cleaning a dump truck and then filling it with dirt. There was no stopping and it was back to work again.

Flying was the easy part. Taking off and heading for the sky was always exciting. The weather made it a bit more nerve racking with high winds, rain and low clouds. The hard part of the flight was the landing. Getting close to the ground brought you in range of enemy gun fire. The L Z itself was always an adventure. They were not prepared landing strips but grassy areas, wooded patches, a clearing in the jungle or a mountain top. This is where the skills of our pilots really showed. They made it look so easy. Listening to the pilots talking to each other and the crew was working to made sure that the landing was safe. These landing were anything but easy.

DOWN IN THE FIELD

On July 4, 1967, we received word that the Marines around Con Thien needed help. They were very close to the Demilitarized Zone (DMZ) that separated North and South Vietnam. The First Battalion Ninth Marines (1/9) had run into a meat grinder. The Marines were outnumbered and had engaged a major North Vietnamese force that was pushing south. They became known as, "The Walking Dead" from the furious and intense fighting. We were to bring in the S.L.F., as we were still aboard the carrier. The battalion would reenforce the other units and join the combat action. We transported 2/3 into L Z Canary, just north of Cam Lo and near Con Thien.

As we made our landing approach to the L Z, on one of the sorties from the ship, my Pilot called to me on the ICS. He said that there was a chip warning light on the Master Caution Panel (MCP). I glanced into the cockpit and could see the yellow warning light on the MCP. I left my gun and began to troubleshoot the chopper. I checked the aft transmission. There were metal chips all over the chip detector. This metal had triggered the warning light. We landed and off loaded our troops. I told the pilot to shut the chopper down. I told him that the chopper was not safe to fly, and the transmission had to be changed. It was tearing itself apart. The pilots left on another chopper, while I stayed with my chopper. My baby, YT 14 was down in the field, but we were alive. The rest of the squadron completed bringing in the battalion into the landing zone, but I wasn't going anywhere. Thanks again Mom for those prayers.

I was in the L Z with my gunner, Carl Yearwood, but I was not afraid. The Second Battalion Third Marines (2/3) surrounded us. We began working on my chopper, dismantling the transmission. Then it was like in the movies, someone yelled, "Saddle up-move em out." The Marines went over the hill and out of sight to find the enemy, that was not far away. I still wasn't scared. I was there with the weapons platoon. They had the heavy machine guns and mortars. Then someone yelled, "Saddle up-move em out." The entire weapons platoon got up and went up over the hill. This left us with seven members of the Naval Forward Observing Gunfire Team. Now, I was both afraid and scared. These guys did not know what they were doing. They were just wandering around the area and were no help to us.

Carl and I continued working on the chopper. We disconnected the engine drive shafts, hydraulic lines and the electrical wiring. This transmission weighed 600 pounds. It is the largest, heaviest single component on the chopper. I had never changed one in the field and I don't think that it had ever been done before. This was a new experience for both of us. Carl's specialty was avionics, namely electronics, but he was a mechanic now! I really didn't have time to worry about these seven guys walking around with .45 caliber pistols on their hips. I didn't have any idea what they were doing out here. I did know that the Viet Cong would love to get their hands on my chopper or me. We all knew that there was a price on the heads of a Pilot or a Crew Chief.

We knew about the pilots that were shot down and captured over North Vietnam. We had flown some search and rescue missions, but not deep into the North. These pilots were tortured and imprisoned, if they were lucky. Some had been killed, even after their capture. There were also choppers that had crashed and burned. Some crews had died, while others were rescued. Some men could not be found and were listed as Missing In Action. Their fate was unknown. Being down in the field was not fun. If Charlie could get his hands on a helicopter or a crew, it would be a big feather in his cap. I was down, but not out.

This was summertime and it was really hot, but the work had to be done. We were sitting in a rice paddy, dried up by the hot sun. This was my chopper and I was going to do my best to get it back to the carrier. I was working on the transmission on the side work platform of the chopper, when I heard a loud boom. I looked over my shoulder and saw where there had been an explosion, with the dust and dirt being blown into the air. There was another boom and I yelled, "In coming." I leaped from the chopper, grabbed my rifle and dove into the ditch at the side of the dried up rice paddy. Carl jumped in next to me. The mortar rounds were still falling and exploding in the nearby field. I said to him, where is your rifle? He had forgotten his rifle, so he ran back to the chopper got it and returned. He had forgotten his bullets and ran back to the chopper. By the time that he had finished running back and forth to the chopper, the mortar rounds had stopped. All of the rounds and explosions had fallen short of the chopper, and there was no damage to it. Now everything stopped. We began preparing our defenses for the night.

We took one of the .50 caliber machine guns out of the chopper and staked it into the ground. We dug a deep foxhole and got ready for the night. From the nearby firebase, they sent us two ambush teams, that were put outside of our perimeter. They gave us some claymore mines and were set up. We were ready for anything that might happen. Here come those Navy guys and they wanted my rifle. I had my rifle, my .38 pistol, and the .50 and I was not giving up any one of them. I might need them. I told them to go over on the other side of the rice paddy, and set up their own perimeter. The sun was going down and it was getting dark. I had been on patrols before, but this was different. We were not near the main base and its defenses. It was darker than I had ever seen it. There were no lights anywhere, the moon was not even out. Pitch black is what they call it. From our position, there were only the two of us. We were alone. There was no one even close to us. We couldn't even see those sailors on the other side of the paddy. We strained to hear anything that might be moving and tried to see into the darkness.

We tried to sleep an hour on and an hour off, while taking turns in keeping watch. This didn't work and we were up all night. We were in our foxhole, and I was leaning on my machine gun. I looked to the tree line and there I saw two Viet Cong soldiers. They were fighting with each other. I decided that I would kill the one that was still standing. Throughout the night they swayed back and forth. They had each other by the throat and were strangling each other. I did not say anything to Carl, but just watched these two. As the morning sun began to rise, I realized that the two Viet Cong soldiers, I watched all night, was actually two trees that were swaying in the breeze. My eyes had been playing tricks on me, all night. This convinced me that I was not going to spend another night out there. I don't even remember seeing those seven sailors after that. I don't know what happened to them or where they went. The chopper was what was important and it was back to work. We had to get my chopper back into flying condition and there was a lot of work still to be done.

In the morning, another transmission was brought out to us. We worked on this all day. How we struggled that 600 lbs. unit out of the chopper and across the dried rice paddy, I will never know. We got it done and installed the new one. I called the ship to have them send two pilots and twenty five gallons of hydraulic fluid, along with some high pressure hydraulic caps. This new transmission did not have a mount for the hydraulic valve locking system, needed for blade folding. I was not worried about this, but the hydraulic lines would pose a problem. I would have to cap them off and might have to bleed air out of the hydraulic system.

With my luck, they had sent everything that I wanted, but with one mistake. They had sent me low pressure caps instead of high pressure caps for the hydraulic lines. This mistake was realized too late to get some more caps. I was not going to spend another night in the field. It was late afternoon when my pilots arrived and began testing the chopper. The Quality

Control Inspector did not come into the field to inspect my work. I said that it was ready to fly. The pilot started the chopper and pulled it into a hover and asked me, how was it in the rear? The sun was going down and it was dark in the chopper. I turned on my flashlight on the rear transmission. It was leaking fluid like a sieve. The low pressure caps could not hold back the fluid in the high pressure lines. I told the pilots that it was okay and to head for the ship.

I told the pilot to fly the chopper with the hydraulic system in isolation. This would cut down on the amount of pressure going to the lines with the low pressure caps on them. I could also refill the system at the same time. As we were flying, I was filling the hydraulic system as fast as I could, as it continued to leak. The pilots never knew the difference, but I told them not to waste any time getting back to the ship. We flew aboard the ship, dripping red hydraulic fluid all over the clean white concrete flight deck of the carrier. The pilots shut the chopper down.

My chopper sat on the flight deck still bleeding red fluid. I still had a few gallons of hydraulic fluid to spare. The guys said that they thought I was still down in the field, I replied that there was no way I was staying there another night, one night was enough. I had been up for more than thirty six hours straight, and had worked my butt off. I was glad to be back aboard the ship. I had lived and was ready to fly for another day. I had brought my chopper, my baby back home. I had to manually fold the rotor blades and park the chopper. Another prayer answered. I took a hot shower and slept like a baby. After completing repairs to my chopper, my flights continued. The Marines had pushed the NVA back across the DMZ, but it would be a long summer battling the enemy around Con Thien. These battles also brought about the use of Surface to Air Missiles (SAM) and rocket propelled grenades (RPG) by the enemy, just another danger added to flying. There were many more flights into this hot area before it was over.

I was working on my chopper aboard the carrier, when we heard an alarm. One of our choppers had taken off and had crashed into the water. We ran to the side of the ship and there it was. We all knew that it could happen, but then again no one ever expects it. All four of the crew had gotten out of the downed bird, before it sank. Things really started to go wrong. The ship could not stop. The sailors got one of their rescue boats started, but it couldn't get into the water. The other boat got into the water but would not start. The Navy's chopper was tied up on the flight deck. We had choppers in the air, but the Navy would not let our choppers handle the rescue. One of our choppers dropped a life raft to the downed crew, but it sank. Our choppers had the capability of landing in the water, but they were not allowed to make a water landing. One of our choppers rescued one crewman by a cable hoist pick up. A chopper responded from Marble Mountain and rescued a second one.

Needless to say, we lost two crewmembers. They all were out of the chopper and floating in the water. There was a big investigation, but it did not satisfy us. Two of our fellow Marines had drowned. Our friends were gone and there were more empty bunks. This ship had a very green and inexperienced crew, and we were salty. It was just the opposite with the crew of the Princeton, when we were green. You can practice for the real thing, but you really don't know for sure about how effective you will be, until the real thing happens and it will definitely happen.

.

We off loaded from this ship. We were glad to get off of it. Our feet were back on dry land and the real fears of combat. We knew that the enemy was trying to kill us. With my swimming skills, I always had the fear of crashing into the water. We did not want to die and especially not by our own negligence. We flew into our new base at Phu Bai. This base was located in the middle of the I Corp region and a few miles south of Hue City. After parking our choppers, we headed for our living area and tried to settle into our new home. We had tents covering the wooden frame hooches again.

It was summertime and was hot and sandy, like being in the desert. We had air conditioning. We were located next to a taxiway and we would open the side of the tent. When a chopper or airplane taxied by, we would let the air blow in. The air wasn't cold, but it was moving. This also let dust and dirt to be blown through the tent. Blowing sand brought the visibility down to near zero. Gritty sand was everywhere - in the bed, in the aircraft, and in the food. Sandy grit was even in the mashed potatoes. There was a crunch when you chewed them. There was absolutely no way of getting away from it. We drank gallons of iced tea to wash the food down. Most of the time there was no ice, but the tea was wet. Well, the food didn't kill us. You can really get spoiled by being aboard the carrier. The combat flights continued without missing a beat.

The maintenance and inspections on the helicopters continued, regardless of the weather conditions. With heavy rains falling, we walked through the thick mud to the flight line. All of the choppers could not fit into the hangers. We worked on the choppers wherever they were, to keep them ready to fly. Work by the ground crew never stopped. The mechanics, metal smiths, hydraulics and electronic personnel were very busy. All of these people were needed to get the choppers into the air. Many times the working conditions were miserable. We would have to adapt and overcome. Sometimes, we were soaking wet or burning up in the hot sun. The comforts of civilization were now gone and we were back to being Marines again.

UPS AND DOWNS

We had flown into the base at Phu Bai and the squadron was going to have a beer party. I had work to do on my chopper and to have it ready for a test flight in the morning. I finished the work in the evening and I told my first mechanic to take the flight. I went to the party and had a good time. I slept late in the morning. It was about eleven in the morning, when I got to the flight line. All of my flight equipment was sitting outside of the maintenance office. I was told that the Commanding Officer wanted to see me. I reported to him and he told me that I was no longer on flight status. I asked why and was told that my chopper was not ready for a test flight this morning. I told him that it was. I had signed off on it the night before and my first mechanic was taking it on a test flight in the morning. This did not make any difference. It was my responsibility. There was no arguing and I never really got an explanation. I was now a mechanic again and would be working on the flight line, as I thought. Well, I was wrong again. He assigned me to mess duty. I reported to the mess hall and asked the Mess Sergeant if I could work the night shift. He said that was fine. Figuring that when the rockets and mortars were going to be exploding, I would rather be awake than sleeping. We were never hit in the daytime.

Well, here I was a crew chief and on mess duty. There really wasn't anyone that I could plead my case to. I did know that there was somebody there that didn't like me. Who was it? Why were they doing this to me? I would do as I was told. I made spam sandwiches, hundreds and hundreds of them. They were for the guys on guard duty and people working on the flight line during the night that needed to eat. I would watch the choppers taking off and landing, during the day and night. They had taken away the one thing that I loved doing, that was flying and that meant being a part of the flight crew. Who said that life was going to be fair? I followed my orders and did my job, whatever it was.

I also had to fill sandbags as part of my punishment. I figured that I would make our own bunker, just outside of our hooch. I dug the hole and filled the bags, but there was no roof on it. The hole got deeper while the walls got higher. Well, it had been raining heavily all day and that night the siren went off. Someone yelled, "In Coming." There were explosions from the rockets that were hitting the flight line. I hit the floor running and ran to the bunker that I had been working on. I jumped over the sandbagged wall. My knee hit the top sandbag. I fell into the bunker landing on my back in about three feet of water. The sandbag followed me, landing on top of me. I nearly drowned, as it held me under water. I was more worried about drowning than being blown up. The next day, I emptied all of the sandbags and filled in the hole. No one ever said anything about it, either.

I was working one night in the mess hall making the sandwiches when the siren went off. The rockets began to fall on the base. We were getting hit and I turned to run for the bunker. Someone turned off the lights. I tripped over some chairs and tables, and landed on the floor. I began crawling toward the door. The explosions got louder, while I was on my hands and knees. The floor was shaking with each explosion. I never did get to the bunker, when the rockets stopped falling. When the lights came back on, and I got up. I continued with making sandwiches, Spam sandwiches. There were thousands of them.

Well that was the rest of my month, mess duty. We lost a whole chopper. This means one thing, we had lost an entire crew, which is four Marines. Was it a mechanical problem, pilot error or enemy action? I wondered if it would have been different, if I was on that flight. Again there were more empty cots, lockers, and faces that we would never see again. There was a feeling of helplessness, because there was nothing that could be done to do to bring our friends back and it still hurt. There was the ever unanswered question, Why did they have to die?

A Vietnamese worker, who was a friend, came up to me and said that we were going to get hit that night and for me to sleep in the bunker. So I went and told our Intelligence Officer. He said that we were not going to be hit and not to worry about it. I thought that he knew what he was talking about. That night, I went to bed and fell asleep. In the middle of the night came the siren and the sound of explosions. Somebody yelled, "In-Coming." It was another mad dash for the bunkers. It was a mortar attack. No one was hurt, but I learned to listen to the workers as they knew what was going on. We would laugh at the Vietnamese workers when they were moving slowly, during the day. We would ask them, "What were you doing humping rockets all night?" They really didn't understand what we were saying. They would smile and shake their heads at us. Chances were very good that they were. No one knew what the enemy looked like or where they were. What a hell of a way to fight a war!

Neatenize - It was the word for making everything nice and neat. We had to rake the sand around the tents. This made each tent have a sense of uniformity, at least the sand was neat. It was anything to keep us busy and our minds off of what was happening around us in Vietnam.

The word came down that there was going to be a raid on Ashau Valley. We were going to be the lead squadron, taking Marines from 2/3 to the top of the valley. We were the senior squadron on the base. Everyone would be flying. There was not going to be any medevacs. The Marines were going to run through and kill every Viet Cong in sight. Ashau Valley was the playground for the Viet Cong and was their rest area. Everyone knew that they were there. This valley was considered to be a No Man's Land. Any aircraft with any bombs left from their missions just dropped them into the valley. We had gotten to know the guys from 2/3 from the other operations. The word was that the first wave of choppers would be blown out of the sky, before they could even land. Now, there is something to look forward to! Being the senior squadron on the base, we had the honor of leading the first wave of the assault. Why worry about it! You know what this means --- PARTY.

We started drinking with the grunts. We knew that tomorrow was going to be our last day on this Earth. It was like being with General Custer at the Little Big Horn River. We knew that the enemy was there, but how many were there? The choppers were ready and so were we. At about midnight, the word came that a jet reconnaissance aircraft had flown into the valley to take pictures. It had been shot up by radar controlled machine guns, but returned to its base. The mission was called off, so we got drunker because we were going to live.

There were many, many drinking parties. Many a morning, we would wake up and be hung over. We would pre-flight our aircraft and do our missions. Sometimes, we didn't feel like flying, but we had a job to do. There were also drugs. At this time, the only one that I saw was Marijuana. Kids would walk up to you with a bag of regular cigarettes containing Pot. They came filtered and unfiltered and the only cost was $5.00 for the bag. I was a drinker, however one night; I had a cigarette that was filled with pot. I wasn't flying, so I took some drags and held them in. I became light headed and everything was funny.

Suddenly the sirens went off and we raced to the bunkers. The base was being hit by rockets. For some unknown reason, I decided that I wanted a rocket. I left the safety of the bunker and headed for the flight line. I was going to catch me a rocket. If I did catch one, I don't know what I was going to do with it. I guess that was an after thought. There were explosions all up and down the flight line. I was knocked to the ground by the concussion of one of the rockets going off. This will sober you up really fast. I made my way back to the hooch after the attack ended. Some of the guys were laughing at me and wondering if I had caught my rocket. I had learned a very quick lesson. Never mess with anything that you can't control. There were many more nights of drinking. I guess that you can call it — anyway to get through the night. A flight crew has to be in control of their own minds and actions at all times, because our lives depended upon it. There is no room for dope. This was not for me. It was also my first and last time trying to smoke pot.

Speaking of defective equipment, in the middle of the summer of 1967, we had a slight problem with our choppers. It was a small problem; the back end of the choppers began to fall off. Cracks were developing in the aft pylon area and the rear rotors would depart from the plane. The chopper really didn't fly without it. One CH-46 chopper landed on the runway and the rear end fell off, while another chopper tore itself apart in a protective revetment. Still, other squadrons had helicopters to fall apart in flight; needless to say, everyone on board was killed. We were flying the choppers harder and longer than what they were designed for. You can make a piece of equipment. How do you really know how it will perform in wartime conditions? You can estimate what the stresses and the loads on the chopper will be. You really don't know the consequences are until the actual situations occur, especially when you are being shot at. This problem became known as the Station 410 Structural Failure. This section of the helicopter had to be strengthened. Well, our choppers were grounded until the problem was fixed. They were sent to Okinawa for the repairs Some of our pilots flew in the older CH-34 piston driven helicopters in other squadrons. Too many good Marines died from this defect.

August 1967 in Phu Bai, I left the mess hall and went to my next assignment. I would be going back to the flight line as a mechanic. Wrong again, I was now assigned to laying concrete with the Navy's Sea Bees. They were making the base bigger. An Army Huey helicopter squadron arrived to help support operations in the area. After a couple of weeks, it was onto interior guard duty for me. There were guard posts around the exterior of the base. My assignment was to guard the helicopters and sleeping areas at night. I was later stationed at the gate on the road leading into the base. There was only a little one man guard shack at this post. I looked around and thought, if we get hit, there is no protection here for me. I took out a shovel and began to dig a fighting hole, next to the shack. The hole was about four feet deep and big enough for me to squeeze into. Well that night, the explosions started going off. We were getting hit again. I jumped into my hole and prepared to defend my position. While the mortar rounds fell, bullets from the Republic of South Vietnam Army (ARVNS) camp at the end of the runaway came flying in our direction. They were supposed to be on our side. They were shooting at us. We always believed that half of them were the enemy anyway.

After the shelling and shooting stopped, I grabbed my rifle and jumped out of the hole. When I did this, I caught my left hand on some of the barred wire fencing and received a cut on my hand. The attack was over and I wrapped my bleeding hand and continued my guard duty. In the morning, I went to sick bay (hospital tent) to have my injured hand treated. The corpsman said that I could get a Purple Heart Medal for the injury. I told him that there were people really getting wounded and killed getting that medal. I told him that I didn't want it. Give it to those that deserve it. I don't rate it. I walked out of sick bay. I had suffered more serious injuries by simply working on the choppers. What kind of life was this for a Crew Chief to be living? I loved flying and being off of the ground really made me feel alive. I was trained to fix helicopters and a qualified crew member. All of this seemed to me to be a waste of my talent. The saying was, "Swing with the Wing". I was not a ground pounder. This being on the ground was for the Grunts. This duty made me feel like I was only trying to exist and not a part of the squadron.

We lost six guys and several more were wounded, during the months of July and August in 1967.

The squadron was still flying and I was still grounded. I was not very happy not flying. Then again, who said that you were supposed to be happy in combat? I was still assigned to guard duty. I slept in the hooch area with the members of the squadron, but that was it. I was working nights and when I came in, the guys were leaving for the flight line. Someone had really tried to remove me as far away as possible from the flight crews, but that was impossible. The feelings that we had for each other would never leave, no matter where we were. There was an emotional bond, a deep sense of camaraderie between each other and a devotion to duty that was beyond belief. "If I have to explain it, then you wouldn't understand it."

REST AND RECUPERATION - (R. & R.)

Along came September 1967, I returned to the squadron and was working again as a mechanic on the flight line. It was my turn for R. & R. and I was going to Bangkok, Thailand. There was a degree of excitement that flowed through my body. I had been writing to Mabel, the entire time that I was in Vietnam. I figured that I would get her an engagement ring, while I was there. Getting back to the world and getting off of life's merry-go-round was what I wanted to do. I thought that I wanted the American Dream. The dream was to get home, get married, and have children and to settle down living the life of a regular American. I guess that I just had seen and done too much. War makes you appreciate life more than ever. You learn very quickly how to enjoy today because tomorrow is promised to no one. I just wanted to relax and be happy.

Just before leaving for Bangkok, I received a letter from Mabel. She stated that she felt that I was a restriction on her social life. What social life? She was in Waterbury and not New York City. She wanted to break up with me. She had made her decision. This was a Dear John Letter and there was nothing else to say. No one ever wanted to receive this type of letter. I really didn't have the time to worry about it. I was too far away and there was nothing that I could do about it. This letter just pulled the rug out from under me and flipped my world upside down. I had a deep hurting and sinking feeling that came over me. I had seen other guys go crazy after receiving this type of letter. I knew that the same thing was not going to happen to me. I could not understand how someone could write such a letter, while you were ducking, hiding and trying to stay alive and to get back home. I just closed that chapter of my life. I was just glad that the letter had come before I bought the ring. The letter also told me what the folks back home thought about us. It was like we didn't really exist or that we were on another planet.

I packed up my gear and headed for the airbase at DaNang. I flew into Thailand. After all of the formalities, I headed for the hotel. The first thing that you do is pay for the room for the five days. If you blow all of your money, at least you would have a place to sleep. I then called home. Mom answered the phone. She then put my Father on. Dad was always straight to the point. Dad said, "Are you all right? Do you need anything? Don't talk too long!" I later learned that the call from the Philippines had costed $126.00. This call was limited to six minutes but still costed $30.00.

After letting them know where I was and that all was well, it was off to the land of the Orient and beautiful women. I had signed up for several tours of the city. I saw the walking Buddha, the talking Buddha, the standing, lying Buddha. I saw more than enough statues of Buddha to last a lifetime. There was the temple tour and Thai boxing. I must admit it, that the women of Thailand are some of the most beautiful in the world and would do anything to please their man. From an early age until adulthood, they learned all there was to know about pleasing a man. There were no thoughts of my former girlfriend. Life was short and I was going to enjoy it as best that I could.

The first day, I went to the New York Cafe. It seemed like no matter what country that we went to, there was always a New York Cafe or Bar. I opened the door and walked in. It was a little dark, but a guy asked me if I wanted a drink, and I replied yes. He sat me down at a table and brought me a rum and coke. I was watching the ladies dancing on the floor. The same man came back to me and he asked if I wanted a girl, and I replied sure. He said pick one. At this time I noticed that all of the women were wearing numbers. I asked for a number and the girl came over. We talked, but I really didn't like her. So, I picked another girl and then another. After several drinks, I came up with one woman that I liked. I had to pay the bar, and she was mine, at least for the night. I went back to the bar the next night and paid for a couple more nights. I learned that the girls could not steal from you or take you to get ripped off. If they did, they would be black balled and could not work in Bangkok. This girl touched my face and said that my skin was the same as Thai, my face was the same as Thai. She then touched my hair and said, " No, same same Thai". We both laughed. It was wonderful to spend time with a pretty girl in a safe place after such a long time. There was no telling how old she was, but she was sexy. We danced, drank and enjoyed each other. She had learned her lessons very well and I was very well pleased.

Well, this girl that I had picked, stayed with me. I told her that I wanted to find a good jewelry store. She took me to the Star of Siam Jewelry Store. There, I drew a picture of a family ring that I wanted made. I was told that it would be ready the next day. We picked up the ring and a tie tack the next day. I paid $32.00 American Dollars for them. When the ratio is 20 of their dollars to one of ours, you could be rich with very little money. I don't know why they call it R & R, because there was no rest or recuperation. It should be I & I, for Intoxication and Intercourse. That is all that was done. It was a real learning experience and I loved it.

During my stay there, I met up with a guy that I knew from Waterbury. He was stationed there with the Army and living in a hotel. Would you believe that some of his friends wanted to take my place on the airplane going back to Vietnam? They must have been crazy to want to leave a paradise for combat. Well maybe there is such a thing of having too much of a good thing, like a kid in a candy store. I didn't want to leave. Any more than five days, I think that it would have killed me. What a way to go! Those five days flew by, for what I can remember of them. It was a quick flight back to Vietnam. I really didn't think about the war and what I was returning to.

It was back to reality and the squadron. I guess you could say that I was refreshed. It was more like being spoiled and tired. Talk about wine, women and song, well Bangkok had them all and it is the real Jewel of the Orient. When I got back to Phu Bai, I found my hooch a little airy. The night before I arrived, we were hit by rockets. This time Charlie came too close. One of the rockets landed in the hooch next to mine and exploded. Needless to say, the entire hooch was blown away. Everyone had gotten into the bunkers before it was hit. My tent cover was in shreds on the side of the blast. The guys were good enough to leave pieces of shrapnel lying on my cot. The blast ruined my speakers in my tape recorder. It was a ugly reminder of what I had missed, but I had really lived at least for five days.

It was now October 1967, and I was becoming a short timer. This meant that I had less that 90 days left to do in Vietnam. Yes, we counted the days left to our tour of duty in this land. This also meant you had to drink a bottle of Seagram VO Whiskey and take the little yellow and black ribbon from around the bottle. This ribbon was placed into the two vent holes in the side of your cover (hat). This would tell everyone that you were a short timer. It was just another drunken night for me. Who said that we were very smart? Somehow this tradition was started and we kept it going.

I was working as a mechanic on the flight line again. I stood on the flight line and watched another Crew Chief, Cisco Martinez flying down the runway, with the last chopper from my section. This meant that I could rest a bit before working on other choppers. Cisco had the nickname of "Injun" and he carried his tomahawk with him on every flight. As the chopper gained altitude, it suddenly slowed down and began to dip and rise. There was something wrong. It looked like the pilots were trying to return to the base. They were in trouble. There was a sense of fear that came over us, as we watching the chopper limp back towards the runway.

Everything seemed to be in slow motion. The chopper continued to lose altitude, while making a slow turn to the right. We all knew there was wrong something. The chopper almost made it to the runway, when it crashed into the field just beyond the airstrip. There was a big cloud of dust and dirt that was thrown into the air, as the chopper met the ground. We had laughed many times sarcastically about crashing, burning and dying in flames. It was unfolding right before our eyes. There was no fire in this crash. We ran down the road to the site of the crash and the barred wire fencing. The crew was getting out of the downed chopper. We were going to help them when another Marine said that they had crashed in the minefield. The chopper did not set off any of the mines. Cisco was helping one of the pilots cross the field to the wire. We passed the injured crewmembers over the barred wired and laid them on the roadside. Ambulances arrived to transport them to the hospital. Cisco then went back to help the other crewmembers. When he learned that he had been walking in a minefield, he almost fainted. The chopper had lost power on an engine on takeoff and that is the worst time, because you are flying low and slow. There really isn't much time to react to the situation. Cisco's chopper was a total loss, but we used a lot of its' parts on other aircraft. Luckily, everyone onboard was injured but they had survived the crash.

At the south end of the runway at the base at Phu Bai was a Viet Cong soldier. Everyone knew he was there. We called him, "One Shot Charlie." We felt that he was issued one bullet per week. When an aircraft would fly over him, he would come out of hiding and shoot it. One of our choppers took off and One Shot Charlie pulled out his rifle and put a bullet through the chopper. No one was hit onboard. The chopper returned to the base to repair the damage. The holes were fixed and the chopper went on a test flight. The chopper passed over the south end of the runway and there was one shot. The bullet struck the chopper again. It was downed for repairs again.

On another occasion, an Air Force C-130 cargo aircraft flew into the base. The plane landed and the pilot reversed his engines to slow the aircraft, as it touched down on the runway. When he did this, one of his four engines burst into flames with burning fuel pouring onto the concrete runway. The crash crew put out the fire. Upon checking the engine, there was a bullet found in the fuel control unit of the engine. One Shot Charlie had struck again. They sent out patrols and ambushes to find him, but they never found him. When they left the area, One Shot Charlie would again do his thing. He used his one bullet very carefully and wisely.

BACK INTO THE AIR

I was working on the flight line, when Captain David Caldon, who was a pilot and the Maintenance Officer, approached me. I learned that his family was from Cheshire, Ct., but he was now living in Maine. He asked me why I was not flying. I told him what had happened to me back in July. He asked me about how much time that I had left to do and I told him. There was a shortage of crew chiefs. I knew that we were going to be short of experienced crewmembers, once we started to rotate back to the States. He said that if I extended my tour of duty in Vietnam, he could get me back on flight status. After spending so many months on the ground, I was given another chance to fly. There was nothing that I loved better than flying and being a member of a combat flight crew. I told him that I would think about it. I went back to the tent area and talked to the other crew chiefs. I learned that they were extending their tour of duty in country. Well, they were not going to stay there without me. Eighteen of approximately 30 Crew Chiefs were staying. I went back to the Captain. I had made my decision and told him that I wanted to extend my tour in Vietnam for another six months. He took out the extension papers and I signed them. I knew that I was being used for my talent, but I did not care.

The Captain kept his word and he put me back on flight status. I had spent too many months on the ground, through not fault of my own. I was back in the air and doing what I loved. I felt like I was alive again. My chopper was YT 3. The job was still pressure filled and the flying was constant, but I was in my glory. On one flight, Captain Caldon was my pilot. Don Clock, who was from Short Beach, Ct., was my gunner. For that day, I renamed my chopper, "The Connecticut Yankee." I also prayed that nothing would happen, because there were three of the four man crew that was from the same state onboard this chopper. It would have been like having three brothers on the same plane. We flew the entire day doing resupply missions, without incident.

Our squadron had made a troop lift and the insertion of a SOG team with a mission across the fence into Laos. One of our choppers had a mechanical problem and it was down in the field. A recovery team, consisting of some of our squadron members, was sent out to recover the chopper. Well, the NVA was there in force. There were approximately 100 Chinese mercenaries and a few Green Berets. They had stumbled into a major enemy force and were heavily outnumbered. The enemy was after them and they needed an immediate extraction, but the weather was really bad. We could not get into the valley and the sun was going down. We sat around our choppers waiting for the weather to clear, but it didn't.

We were told that if we didn't get them out by a certain time, we could write all of them off as being killed in action. Everyone became edgy, as we watched the clock. The time came and went. A cloud of depression settled in over the squadron. We left the flight line and went to the Enlisted Men's Club. There we began to drink to our lost squadron mates. They had gone to do a mission, to do a job and now they were gone. It was a very sad night. There were no tears, just drinking and remembering the good times that we all had shared. It was our way of grieving. Drinks were raised, toasts were made and we sang songs to our lost squadron mates.

When the morning sun rose, we were told that our friends were still alive and we were going to get them. There was a sudden surge of hope and happiness that ran throughout the entire squadron, as we readied our choppers for the flight. We manned our aircraft and took off. We were heading for the fence, namely the border. The sky was still full of white fluffy clouds, as the squadron flew over them. Out of the sea of clouds was just one hole. Through this hole in the clouds, chopper after chopper dove down towards the valley below.

We landed and picked up all of the troops and flew them back across the fence to the safety of Vietnam. If you can call it a safe place. Well, it was safer than running around in the jungle.

Our squadron mates said that they had destroyed the chopper to keep it out of the enemy's hands. All night long the enemy had chased them around through the jungle. Air strikes and artillery had saved them. They had looked up in the morning at the sky. The entire sky was still covered with low hanging gray clouds. They had seen the single hole in the clouds and watched as the 46's came diving through it. They said that the choppers looked like angels descending to get them. They knew that we were coming for them. We told them about the drinking party that we had the night before for them. Now it was time for another party, because they were alive and back with us.

Thanksgiving came and we were still flying. We delivered special hot turkey dinners to the troops in the field. We even delivered ice cream and it wasn't melted when it arrived. There were no such things as holidays for us. We worked seven days a week. There were no days off and there was always something that had to be done. If we weren't flying, we were doing maintenance on the choppers. We flew in all types of weather, because we had all weather capabilities. We continued to maintain the reputation that if "You called and we hauled it". We would be there.

In December 1967, it was party time. Marines that I had landed with in Vietnam of HMM-262 and were transferred into HMM-164, were rotating back to the States. Their time was up and they were heading home. I was going to miss them. The laughs, jokes and fun that we had would be over. I was staying, along with the other crew chiefs. The original members of HMM-262 were also going home. I began to think that I might have made a mistake by extending my tour.

They were leaving and I could have been going with them. My Brothers were going home and they would be missed. There were no tears and never a thought that we would not be seeing each other again. We were happy for those that were leaving. I guess it was just the wrong time of the year. It was the monsoon season again and it was raining. Day after day, no sun, low clouds and plenty of rain, but the flights and work went on. Personnel were being transferred into the squadron at different intervals. This was done so there would not be another depletion and shortage of pilots or crew chiefs.

I was also spending my second Christmas in Vietnam. It was colder and still raining, as usual. This time there was no red clay. We had white sand. The sand just turned into a mush. We were further north this time. It did not snow, but it was definitely cold. There was still a degree of sadness of not being at home with family and friends. This feeling was short lived, because we were with our other family. We were fighting to stay alive, protecting and caring for our brothers in arms. We were flying almost every day and night as the war went on.

As for Captain Caldon, I returned from a day's missions and learned that he had been transferred to Khe Sanh, as a Forward Air Controller (FAC). He would coordinate the air support for the base. Now this did not make any sense to me. Here is a chopper pilot with rank and they are sending him to the farthest and most dangerous outpost that we had. He was gone and I would miss him. He would later be awarded the Silver Star for his actions there. He became known to us, as our "Super Grunt". I personally believe that it was done, because he had placed me back on flight status. There was no way of proving it. There were some White Marines of assorted ranks that didn't like me telling them what to do. It didn't bother me, as long as they did what I told them to do. The maintenance on the helicopter would be done to my satisfaction. Being the Crew Chief gave you this kind of power. It was my chopper, my responsibility and I was flying in it.

I had spent the entire year of 1967 in Vietnam and it was now January 1968. I had made it through to another New Year's Eve. It was another uneventful night of pop up flares going off to bring the New Year. I guess with over a year of service in country, and I had become a veteran. Some more guys were being rotated home, while the crazy Crew Chiefs kept on flying and holding the squadron together. As I think back on those times, I really can't figure out, who didn't like me or why they disliked me, but there was definitely someone. Could I have been so naive? It seemed like every dirty job was given to me. I did my job, whatever it was.

At this time, I was thinking more about going home for my thirty day leave. I needed to make a leg run to a small village outside of Hue City. I jumped onto the garbage truck and got off in town. This was Highway One and it led to the old Provincial Capital of Hue City. There was something unusual about this trip. I noticed there were no young men in the village. This did not stop me. A kid came up to me and asked, do you want a girl? My sister is number one. This kid led me to a hut and there I found his sister. She was lying on the bed. I undressed and I placed my .38 pistol along the side of the pillow. If you really want to call this the missionary position, I guess this was it. You never trusted these little villages and never knowing who else might be around. For some reason, I could not reach a climax, so the sex went on for a while, a good long while. After taking care of business and paying her, she said to me, "Next time you come, I get you dog." I signaled a garbage truck to stop. Feeling rejuvenated, I rode back to the base.

There was something else that was strange. We had flown missions to insert senors into several areas along the border, that were heavily traveled by the enemy. These senors would detect enemy movement and send a signal back to a military headquarters. Air strikes and artillery shells would be sent into the area to assault the enemy troops. The Intelligence Section of our squadron said that they had been tracking two hundred trucks that were coming down the Ho Chi Minh Trail, heading for South Vietnam. Somehow they lost them. Now how do you lose two hundred trucks? This was supposed to be a war, why didn't they just blast them? I was told that they wanted to see where they were going. What a funny way to fight a war! Well, I wasn't worried about it. I was thinking about the trip home for my leave. I would later learn that those trucks turned up outside of the City of Hue, during the Tet Offensive, a few weeks later.

COMING HOME - 1968

I left Vietnam on January 17th, from the airport at DaNang. After a stopover in Okinawa, it was onto Travis Air Force Base, California. I had to stop by Vallejo, Calif., to visit the family of Lonnie Clark, before coming home. Lonnie was another Black Marine, from my squadron and was a flying Crew Chief. There were only four of us in the squadron. He had asked me to see them for him. I caught a bus to his hometown. There I met his brothers, sisters and his parents. I spent the day with them. They were very pleased that I did stop by. Lonnie was fine and doing his job. I explained the job that we were doing. They were very proud of him. They treated me just like family. I thanked them for their kindness. I told them that I would be returning to Vietnam and would be seeing Lonnie again. They expressed their love for him and thanked me for stopping to see them. Lonnie's brother drove me to the airport and I caught my flight to New York. The thoughts of seeing my family and the anticipation of getting home was growing. I had a sense of excitement from being away from home for over a year. When I arrived at the airport terminal in New York, I needed a pack of cigarettes, so I bought one at the concession stand. It costed fifty one cents. This was outrageous. I vowed that I would never pay that much for cigarettes again.

It was late when I arrived in New York. I walked over to the car rental phones. Picking up the receiver, I said, " I would like to rent a car". The person on the other end asked, "Do you have a credit card?" I said No. They replied then we can't rent you a car without one. After being told the same thing from the different companies, I was getting hot. I told them that I just back from Vietnam and I only had hard cold cash money in my pocket. They didn't care. I needed a credit card. Who needed or even had a credit card in Vietnam? I had gotten all the way to New York and couldn't get home, that was just 100 miles away. I took a cab to the bus station. The last bus had left for the night, so I wandered around the terminal. I looked at the people lying on benches and sleeping on the floor. I thought about how nice it was to just sleep without the worry of somebody dropping rockets on them. What a blessing! I was so close to getting home. I would have to wait for the sun to come up. I caught the first bus for home, in the morning.

I walked into the house and there were plenty of hugs and kisses. They all were happy to see me. At least until I told my parents that I was going back. This really pissed off my father. I tried to explain why I extended my tour there, but he didn't want to listen. All that he said was, "You Damn Dummy!" He just walked away from me. I knew that it was hard on my mother with me being over there, but I think that it was even harder on my father. He would never admit it. Everyone talks about their mothers' feelings, but fathers have feelings too. He had been in combat during World War II in Europe and he knew what combat was like. He never talked about his combat experiences, but he must have had some fears for me and my safety.

I knew that I had a year and a half left to do with my enlistment and I was promised only six months in the States. After that I could be sent back to Vietnam for another year. I was already there and knew the feelings of being there. I didn't want to come to the states and then be shipped back there. I guess by staying, I was beating them out of six months in combat. I guess that there was a method to my madness. My job as a Crew Chief was considered to be a critical job. There was also the point of staying with my second family. My explanation didn't make a bit of difference or sense to them. My parents were wondering where had they gone wrong. Their son wanted to return to a place, where he could get killed as opposed to being here, where it was safe. All that they knew was that I was going back to that place called Vietnam. I was just a Dummy!

I went to see my former girlfriend, the one that had written me the DEAR JOHN LETTER, saying I was a restriction on her social life. What social life? I talked to her and stated that I wanted to do something for her, since she had written to me for almost a year. She did not want anything, but I insisted. I told her that I had bought her a new color television. She told all of her friends and they must have thought that I was crazy or some kind of a nut. I carried this story on for a week. Well, when I told her that I didn't buy it. She started to cry and said what am I going to tell my friends? That was her problem and her social life. There was no arguing. I turned and walked out of the door, without looking back.

I was sitting on the couch at home and turned on the television. The Battle for Khe Sanh had started, as well as the Tet Offensive. The entire country of Vietnam had exploded all at once. From one end of the country to the other, the Viet Cong and the NVA were attacking everything. It was all right there, the war in my living room. I watched my squadron going into action without me. The big white Y T on the choppers was easy to see on the television screen. It was a short news clip. I was not supposed to be sitting there, I was supposed to be flying with them. My brothers needed me. I had some of my fun while I was at home. I must admit it that my heart was in Vietnam and there was some guilt about watching the war on television and not being there. Where was I supposed to be? This might sound crazy, but it was true. There is no way to explain it, you would have to have been there and feel the sense of devotion that we had for each other. Being at home again, I had a strange feeling and felt like a fish out of water.

It was January and very cold. I had actually missed the ice and snow of winter. I walked up the hill to my parents' house. From the first floor window there was a funny looking thing hanging on the clothesline. It was frozen stiff and was the only thing on the line. As I got closer, I saw what it was. It was my Give-A- Shit Hat. It was my jungle hat that was not military issue and a symbol of my attitude. My mother had washed it. It took me a year to get it dirty. Now I would have to start all over. I guess that you get a little superstitious being in combat. My hat was lucky for me, while I was over there. It was not so lucky when my mother got her hands on it. The local newspaper even interviewed me about the war. I gave them my prospective. It was not what they wanted to hear. I explained our mission there and what we were doing. I was proud of what I was doing. I had missed most of the anti- war sentiment by being over there and not here. What did they really expect to hear from a Marine in combat? The reporter put in a sarcastic comment into the article. He stated that we would see about my views, if I returned from Vietnam. Well, this thought never entered my mind.

I started dating a new girlfriend and we went to the movies. It was the State Theater on East Main Street and the movie was "The Green Berets" starring John "The Duke" Wayne. It was a pro-Vietnam movie that had just been released. I was sitting there and laughing at some of the scenes. They looked like pure Hollywood and not reality. In one scene a helicopter is shot down. It was on fire and crashed. The chopper rolled over throwing the Duke and one crew member clear of the burning wreckage.

Naturally, John Wayne was okay, but the Crew Chief came out of the chopper and he was on fire. I laughed and said that was me, as I pointed at the screen. Well, the movie ended. An elderly lady looked at me with anger in her eyes. She had heard me laughing. She said how could I laugh at the movie, when our boys were over there dying. I replied to her, I had just gotten back from there and was going back. I think she thought that I was lying, as she walked up the aisle away from me, shaking her head.

Now, it was the middle of February and time for me to leave again. I told Mom to keep on praying. I really couldn't wait to get back to Vietnam and my friends. It was like living in two different worlds. The brothers that I served with were closer to me than my own brothers and I loved them, just as much. You wouldn't understand it, if you weren't there. My parents saw me off again. There was no telling what thoughts were going through Dad's mind. I went to New York and boarded a plane and flew to San Francisco. Then it was onto Okinawa and then to DaNang. This trip seemed faster and it really didn't take very long to get back.

Upon arriving back at Phu Bai, I learned the awful truth. Lonnie had been killed a few days earlier. Could this have been the reason why I was in such a hurry to get back? I really don't know. Lonnie had been flying over Hue City, when he was shot. He always wore his bullet bouncer, but not on this mission. I was crushed by this news. I had a deep sinking feeling that hurt me to the core of my being. Another member of my Marine Family, my friend and brother had died and I wasn't there for his memorial service. Lonnie was happy and full of life. I had last seen his parents a month earlier and everything was fine. I told them what Lonnie had told me to tell them. Now, he was gone and I would never see his face again. Lonnie loved flying and being a part of a flight crew. The two other Black Crew Chiefs had quit flying, while I was at home. Something had happened while I was gone, but I can't remember what it was now. I know that they tried to get me to quit flying too. I had a decision to make.

I loved flying and liked what I was doing. I always did what I wanted to do and not to follow the crowd. I had to be my own man. I could have taken the easy life. I could have worked as a mechanic on the flight line, drink and have a party at night. There would be no need to be worrying about a morning flight or the responsibility of being in charge of the cabin area, no pressures about the worries about hairy missions, being shot at or even being down in the field, not to mention putting yourself in harm's way.

I had decided that I would continue flying. Sometimes I think that I should have listened to them and quit. Then again, I don't think that I would have been happy with myself, if I had. I was still assigned to YT - 3, as my chopper, my baby. I renamed it as Tina's Toy, after my new girlfriend. This was my job and my responsibility. I kept on flying. Lonnie and his infectious smile were gone, but his spirit would always there with me. Lonnie would be missed, but never forgotten.

SIEGE ON KHE SANH — TET OFFENSIVE 1968

We were still flying into Khe Sanh, on a daily basis. The Generals had made the decision to defend this base. The base had top priority over every place else in Vietnam, even with the Tet Offensive still going on. Whatever they needed, we brought it to them. When the weather was bad, many times we were the only type of aircraft that could get in and out of there. I had missed some of the fighting, but there was plenty left to go around. The base was surrounded and still under siege, being shelled by rockets and mortar rounds on a 24 hour basis. Charlie also had artillery that was being fired from North Vietnam onto the base. The French forces were defeated in this same manner many years before. It was like being in the Alamo and they were fighting in all directions. You couldn't drive to Khe Sanh, but we certainly could fly in there. Why should the Marines have to take such a pounding? I had spent plenty of nights at this outpost and knew what the Marines were going through. We were not going to let the base fall to the enemy.

Super gaggles were formed. These gaggles consisted of helicopters from several squadrons. Every squadron was doing the same thing at the same time. We all headed to the base with our cargo and troops. The sky was filled with helicopters and it was really crowded. We brought in the ammunition, food, water and whatever else was needed. We would then take out those that were scheduled to leave, along with wounded and the dead. We were also known as magnets. Every time that we came in, we would get the enemy's attention. We attracted enemy rockets and mortar rounds that began to fall on the base, as well as bullets from ground fire, as we approached. The chopper made a steep approach and a quick drop into the L Z. The time on the ground was very limited. If there is a place called Hell on Earth, this was it. The longer we were on the ground, the greater chance we had of being hit. The wreckage of various aircraft that had been destroyed littered the area. The missions to Khe Sanh never stopped. All around the base was nothing but death and destruction.

On one mission into Khe Sanh, as we were approaching the base, I noticed vapor trails going down towards the base. They were from the mortar rounds and rockets raining down onto the base, followed by the explosions. The base was under attack. We circled and waited until there was a lull. We then made our run to the L Z. The pilots had learned to stand the chopper on its end and let the cargo slide out the rear ramp to the ground. I must admit it was a fast way to unload the chopper. I would untie the load. My gunner and I would hold on, so we would not slide out with the cargo while this maneuver was being performed. There was the wreckage a C-130 cargo aircraft that had been hit on the runway and had burned. The Air Force was not landing either. They were making low level cargo extractions, along the runway without stopping. Para-drops were also made over the far end of the base. The cargo plane would fly in low, at about 500 feet above the ground. They pushed the cargo out of the airplane and it would come down by parachutes into the landing area. The ground crew would dodge the explosions to get the much needed supplies.

On another mission, I looked out of the cabin door, while we were making our approach to Khe Sanh. There I saw a C-130 making his run on the base. There was a small parachute that was coming out of the back of the plane. It began pulling the rest of the cargo out of the rear of the transport aircraft. I yelled to the pilot, "Para-drop at 3 o'clock." We banked hard to the left and got out from underneath of the load. A week later, I heard that a chopper from a sister squadron had been run over by one of these cargo drops. This killed all of those on board the chopper. This was just another hazard of flying. There were so many different types of aircraft flying around that small area. There were transports, helicopters, jets, bombers and anything else that would fly. The Marines had first priority for anything that they needed. The 26th Marines were ready and so were the choppers. Marine jets dropped bombs and napalm very close to the base. The B-52 bombing raids had finally broken the backs and the will of the North Vietnamese Soldiers. After 77 long days of intense fighting, the siege on the base was broken.

We didn't know the siege was over, because there were still flights to be made into the area. The fighting continued, but we were now on the offensive. Marine Corps History was made during this stand. The Grunts had been outnumbered and surrounded, but surrender was never a thought or even an option. The looking for the enemy was not a problem, anymore. The North Vietnamese Army had found the Marines and they would pay a heavy price. Those poor Bastards had the Marines surrounded and now what were they going to do with them? The Marines were like a cat backed into a corner. They came out fighting with all of the spirit and tradition that had made the Corps famous. There were many bloody battles fought before the NVA was pushed back across the DMZ into North Vietnam.

I have seen and read several historical accounts of this battle. The credit was given to the Air Force and the Army for breaking the siege. For some reason, the Marine Helicopter Squadrons are not even mentioned. We were there and kept the base supplied with whatever they needed, especially when no one else could. The Marines at Khe Sanh knew that we were there and that is what is important. Our squadron received a Presidential Unit Citation for our participation in this battle.

The Tet Offensive was still under way. We were still flying support for the Marines and South Vietnamese Army fighting for the City of Hue. There were plenty of wounded and dead, during the house to house fighting. The Viet Cong were also learning how to shoot down our choppers. There was no rest for us. There was always another flight to take. The Grunts didn't rest and neither did we. The Grunts thought that we were suicidal for flying around in large sitting ducks. Flying low and slow made us a very inviting target. The fight for Hue City was finally over and the V C were beaten. Throughout the entire country of Vietnam, the forces of North Vietnam and the Viet Cong were defeated. U. S. combat forces did not lose one single major battle during this time. They all fought with honor and distinction. We fought for each other and did our jobs. We did not receive the backing from the home front. We felt like outcasts from society. Back in the States, there was an even louder cry through demonstrations for the end of the war.

We had the least number of deaths of all of the operational Marine Helicopter Squadrons in Vietnam. Every military unit had a motto and ours was — **"Flying Death"**. There was a skull with a bullet hole in it and a vulture sitting on top was painted on the cowling of the forward transmission of each one of our choppers. We could rain death down from the skies with our bullets. We also died trying to help our fellow Marines that needed us. No matter which squadron lost a chopper or a life, every loss hurt us. We were a family.

The Crew --- taken April 8, 1968 aboard the Valley Forge with my 1st mechanic and gunner Michael Gilbert atop YT- 3, with Flying Death Symbol on the forward rotor head.. Rotor blades are folded.

The Squadron again deployed aboard another carrier. This time it was the U.S.S. Valley Forge. It was another round bottomed boat. We floated around the South China Sea. My chopper YT - 3 was sent to overhaul and I was assigned to YT -14, which was brand new. We really needed a rest, even if it was for only at night. This was April 1968 and we heard that Martin Luther King had been killed in Memphis. He was the nonviolent symbol of the civil rights movement. The whole country was going nuts. There was rioting throughout the country and cities were burning. We were reading all of this in the Stars and Stripes Newspaper. There was a filler article on the bottom one of the pages and it said, "Riot in Waterbury Connecticut." Well, all right, the whole world had not passed my hometown by. It was only a couple of lines. We had more pressing problems, like staying alive, and flying our missions. As long as everything was all right with my family. What could I do about it by being so far away? I just had to worry about what I was doing. Race riots and antiwar demonstrations were far removed from us, but we heard about them. The country was redefining its future or it was tearing itself apart. The vast majority of Americans could really care less about those that were doing its country's bidding in Vietnam. We had our own jobs to do and there was no time to worry about what was going on back home.

There were several unusual incidents and close calls that happened to me, as they did with others that were flying. Every Pilot and Crew Chief has stories of what didn't go right on a flight or a mission.

While we were returning from a mission, there was a heavy cloud cover all around. We were flying above the clouds, just off of the coast of Vietnam heading south. We had to drop down through the cloud layer to make our approach to the base. As we broke through into the clear, one of my pilots yelled, "Aircraft at 12 o'clock!" We banked hard to the left, as I looked out of the cabin door. There was a Marine A-4 attack jet coming straight at us. He was banking his plane hard to his left. We passed each other, definitely too close for comfort. I could see his full bomb load, hanging under his wings. With all of the flying and the different types of aircraft, it is a wonder why there weren't more midair collisions. The skills of our pilots got us into enough trouble and those same abilities saved us on more than one occasion, not to mention the prayers.

While returning from one mission, I heard a loud bang that was outside of the chopper. I looked out of the cabin door and up toward the rear rotor blades. There I saw that the rear clamshell access doors had blown open in flight. The locking latches had broken. I had the pilots land. I removed the doors and threw them into the cabin. My copilot said that we could not fly like that. I guess that if the chopper didn't look like it came from the factory, it wasn't safe; at least that is what he thought. I convinced him that it was safe to fly. Our choppers were well worn, but they were as safe as we could make them. We flew back to the ship.

On another mission, we were carrying a Marine Brigadier (one star) General and some of his staff. My wingman radioed that he had a problem and had to land, immediately. As we were following our wingman down, my pilot told me that we had a chip detector warning light on the Master Caution Panel from the transmission. I left my machine gun and began to troubleshoot the chopper. I ran to the rear of the chopper and laid on the ramp to check the aft transmission. The chip detector was okay. I glanced into the cabin area and was surprised to see that the General had jumped from his seat and onto my machine gun, while I was checking out the problem. I then ran forward through the cabin passed him and checked the forward transmission chip detector. It was clear. I then found the problem. I told my pilot and turned the warning light on and off several times. It was only a broken wire that I soon fixed. The warning light went out.

Both choppers landed. The General was looking over my machine gun out of the aircraft. He was covering the right side of my chopper, as we sat in a jungle clearing. My wingman also fixed his problem. We both took off again. It was the first time that I ever had a General take over my gun. I must admit that a General just didn't look right on a machine gun. He smiled and nodded to me, as he returned to his seat. I smiled and returned his nod, as I took over my gun. There was an unspoken, mutual respect that was shared for a moment regardless of rank, but Marine to Marine. This respect felt good. We completed the mission. He was actually under my command while he was my passenger, but I would never tell a General that. Well then again, no matter what your rank is, you are a Marine first and he became my right side machine gunner.

One more mission, we had flown into a loading area. I noticed that we were losing fuel from under the right stub wing fuel tank. I told the pilot that I was going outside to fix the problem. I went out of the back of the aircraft and crawled under the stub wing. There wasn't much room between the ground and the chopper. I was closing the fuel drain at the bottom that was leaking. As I was doing this, the chopper began to rise. I thought that my pilot was picking the chopper up a little, giving me more room to work. My helicopter rose higher and higher. I reached for my intercom button, just as my ICS cord pulled out from my helmet, and the chopper lifted off. There I was lying flat on my back with my hands in the air. I watched my chopper get smaller and smaller, as it went higher and higher. I got a completely different prospective of my chopper, as the rotor wash blew sand and dirt all around. This sight was what the troops would see when I would be leaving the zone. I wasn't going anywhere and felt very strange. How could this happen? They actually left me!

The Marines on the ground in the L Z were laughing and asked me if this happened to me very often. I got to my feet, standing with my hands on my hips, looking skywards. I watched my chopper continue to gain altitude. I shook my head from side to side, in a state of shock and disbelief. They actually left me on the ground. My chopper then turned slowly, making an "S" turn before returning to the L Z. My gunner must have told the pilots that they had left me on the ground. As my helicopter landed, the pilots were laughing. I jumped in through the cabin door. I just looked into the cockpit at them, as I plugged my helmet into the ICS. I was not happy and said, "Very, Very Funny, Don't let it happen again!" We all laughed and took off again. This time it was with a full crew and we completed our mission.

THE ROCKPILE — A FLYING LESSON

I had made many flights to the Rockpile. There was a Marine observation post, located on the top of the 700-foot mountain peak. They would watch for any enemy troop movements in area. The choppers were their lifeline. Everything was flown to them. While flying a resupply mission to the Rockpile, I had a young Second Lieutenant as the copilot aboard and at the controls. The copilot made the approach to the landing pad. The wind was blowing the chopper all over the top of the mountain. We were trying to pick up an external load. I was lying back on the floor by the hellhole with the external hook. Watching the ground crew for signals and I was directing the copilot. We went forwards, backwards, left, right, up and down as we neared the load. We went every way but the right way. I finally yelled for the copilot to hold the chopper steady. The pilot, who was a Captain, took over the controls, brought the chopper around and held it in a hover. The ground crew hooked up the external load of empty water cans to the cargo hook.

The copilot again took over the control. I told him to pick the chopper and load up. The engines needed time to adjust to the added weight and to build up its power, before lifting off. Well, the copilot began to drag the load off of the platform. I kept telling him, up, pick the chopper up, but he didn't. I yelled to the copilot, as the load swung off of the platform. The chopper drooped, rapidly losing altitude. I saw the ground rushing up toward me, as I looked through the hellhole. I screamed as the chopper dropped and accidentally pushed my talk button. My voice went through the ICS and the pilot jumped in his seat. He asked me what was wrong and I replied, "He almost killed us". To this day, I don't know why the rotor blades didn't hit the loading platform. This would have meant certain death. We would have fallen to the floor of the valley, crashing and burning all the way down. There were no parachutes or any time to get out. Another prayer was answered — Thanks Mom.

We flew back to Dong Ha with the external load and dropped it off at the L Z. We then landed and parked the chopper. My Pilot said that he wanted to check out the number 2 engine. I said that I would get the copilot. He told me that I was going to fly the left seat, in the copilot's position. This was a shock to me. I had never sat in that seat before, while we were flying. I jumped into the copilot's seat and strapped in. We flew over to an isolated spot, where he checked out the engine. It was strange for me to be sitting up in front, while we were flying. This was a very different perspective of flying. After several minutes we landed, there was nothing wrong with the engine.

The pilot looked at me and told me to pick the chopper up. I looked over at him and he was serious. I had seen the pilots do this hundreds of times. I put my hands and feet on the flight controls. I pulled the cyclic stick back slightly and began to pull up on the collective stick. I felt the aircraft start to rise. In my mind, I could mentally see the levers, cables and actuators moving to change the pitch on the rotor blades. The chopper was not off of the ground. I pulled in a little more power and I could feel the chopper rising, but we were still on the ground. The flight controls were like driving with power steering. I didn't know exactly how much power to give the chopper. The pilot grabbed the stick and put the chopper into a hover and said, "You've got it". I said that I have the aircraft. After what seems like a few minutes, I asked, "How am I doing?" He replied, not bad but you are swinging back and forth, like a pendulum. I was over correcting with the flight controls. The pilot stopped the chopper and gave the controls back to me. Again, I asked how was I doing and I got the same reply, except this time, I was in a nose down attitude. He told me to pull back on the cyclic stick. I did and we went backwards.

He took the controls and stopped us. The flight controls were very sensitive.

My pilot turned over the controls to me and said head for the river. The river was on the left, so I pulled in some power, push a little left rudder and moved the cyclic stick to the left. We were heading for the river. The pilot asked me about what altitude we started off at and I replied 500 feet. He asked me what altitude I was now at. Glancing at the altimeter, I replied 2,500 feet. We were going up like we were in an elevator. I had pulled in too much power. We flew back to Dong Ha and landed. The pilot said to me that these choppers are not that easy to fly. I agreed that the choppers were difficult to fly. He asked me if I thought that I should apologize to the Lieutenant. Everything that I had said went through the ICS and was heard by the entire flight crew. I had really spoken harshly, in no uncertain terms, about the copilot. I guess that I had embarrassed him. This was not a test flight but a flight lesson for me. I understood the lesson, too. I told him, "No, I don't think so, he is supposed to know how to fly the chopper". My pilot understood what I was talking about and nothing more was ever said.

The operation of this complex flying machine was not easy, but a good crew made it look very easy. We would spiral down into the smallest of L Z's and back into the air. What good am I, if the pilot doesn't listen to me? Mechanically, I knew what it took for a safe flight. I was not being disrespectful, but I was serious. Flying is a serious business and there is very little room for errors or mistakes. Everyone has to be a rookie at sometime. How do you gain experience to learn your way through the hazards of flying? Being the pilot at the controls, you are responsible for not only yourself but the entire crew. Sometimes it costed lives, but not this time.

This was my first time being behind the controls, but not my last. There were several bad incidents had taken place in the cockpits of choppers in other squadrons. Pilots were wounded and killed. The pilots started to believe that the crew chief should have some knowledge of flying the aircraft, in the event of something happening to one or both of the pilots. The crew chiefs got plenty of stick time on test flights. This really did made sense to me. I liked the experience of sitting up front, there was so much that had to be done. I had seen the pilots in action doing their jobs. This time, I was sitting in the hotseat, at the controls and flying this big mechanical machine.

The thought of my being a pilot never entered my mind. This opportunity was never offered to me, while I was growing up. The schooling was that I could work in the factories or be a mechanic. This was the direction that I was led to. There was college, but aviation was not one of the topics mentioned. If a child is not exposed to opportunities that are there, and given the schooling that is needed, then they will never aspire to reach for a higher level. The educational experience is the same about becoming a doctor, lawyer or business person. I knew that I had the knowledge and ability to repair helicopters. Now, I also knew that I could fly one too.

SALTY COMBAT CREW

We were still aboard the ship, the U. S. S. Valley Forge. The food was good, hot showers, and a safe place to sleep. Sailing around the South China Sea, on a helicopter aircraft carrier, what a pleasure, especially for the sailors. It was nice to be on the flight deck in the evening with the cool ocean breezes blowing in your face. This eased and took away a lot of the tension. The flight crews laughed, joked and tried to relax. We were still flying into the country, every day. We faced the perils of combat with confidence of being a normal job. We were tired from the constant flying and maintenance. With the shortage of parts and necessary equipment, we were holding the choppers together on a shoe string. There were fears, but the mission came first.

I had a Second Lieutenant come out to my chopper and he was checking it out before our flight. I guess he thought that he was doing his preflight inspection of the chopper. He was looking at the engines. I knew he did not know what he was doing. This pilot had just come over from the States. He was standing on the ramp and said to me, "What do you think of the outfit?" I replied, "It sucks, Sir". This really got to him. He spouted back, "What! This is still the Marine Corps!" I replied, "Look around you, do these guys look like Marines?" We were all greasy and dirty from working on the choppers. He then said, "This is still a military organization." I said, "Have you been down to the Maintenance Office? There is no organization down there." He had asked me for my opinion. I don't know what answers he was looking for, but my responses were not to his liking. He just shook his head and walked away.

I later found this same Lieutenant. I explained to him that this was war and not the States. We have a different attitude over here. We know what their rank was, their nicknames and respected their rank as Officers, but we are all a part of a team

171

and that is a flight crew. There is mutual respect given to each other, because we depended on and relied on each other. If we had to salute every Officer as they walked by, we would never get any work done. There is a time and place for everything. He understood what I was saying. I told him that if he wanted, I would show him the proper way to pre-flight a chopper. He agreed and I showed him how to pre-flight inspect the chopper and what to look for. I am quite sure that he talked to the veteran pilots and learned how to get along with the flight crews. He became one of our better officers and pilots. I was very salty by this time from being in Vietnam for over a year.

On more than one occasion, incidents would occur while starting the engines. The Crew Chief would respond to the pilot, "Ready on the APP" and waited for the whine of the small jet engine. The whine would rise and then suddenly drop. The Crew Chief would run to the ramp and the hand pump for the hydraulic system. He pushed the handle of the pump as fast as he could. This would replace the pressure in the system to start the engines. With sweat running down his face, the engine would start. I knew my job, but I also had to know about the pilot's job. Yes, the Crew Chief even watched what was going on in the cockpit, too. Flying with the flight gauges in the green, no over revving of the blades or engines and no hard landings, if this happened the Crew Chief was not going to be very happy. There is a lot of maintenance that has to be performed, when the chopper is over stressed. Altitude, airspeed, and a good attitude, along with a good Crew Chief were a Pilot's best friends.

There was talk about the squadron going back to Subic Bay. We were tired and looking forward to some rest and going back to the Philippines. The carrier was going there and the rumors were flying. We began thinking about the women, drinking, and parties there. Then we soon learned that we would be doing all of the flying and would not be going back, but the ship was. Instead the squadron was split up. We were off loading into the bases at Phu Bai and Quang Tri. The ship left without us. We continued flying our missions to support the troops. No time off and just one good deal after another. When the ship returned to the combat area, we again reloaded aboard it. We continued flying our missions, with the precision of a fine watch. The squadron was operating like a well oiled combat machine with seasoned flight crews. The hot showers, good food and quiet nights were welcomed with open arms.

It was now April 1968. There were promotions being handed out, but not for me. I was a Corporal and everyone around me was making Sergeant. I went to find out why I was not being promoted. I was told my conduct and proficiency marks were too low. I checked and found that my last marks were a 4.2 and a 4.3 out of a possible 5.0. All of the rest of my marks had been 4.8, 4.9 and even a couple of 5.0, which was considered to be outstanding. How could this happen? I was a flying Crew Chief, and had extended for another tour in combat, so how could my conduct marks be so low as a 4.2 and my job performance marks be a 4.3? This really did not make any sense to me. I was told that my marks were so low that I would never be promoted to the rank of Sergeant.

My Sergeant Section Leader that gave me the low rating marks had rotated back to the States. This meant that I could not question him about my marks. Why would he give me such low marks? I was told that I could make a complaint to the Commandant of the Marine Corps about it. Like he didn't have enough to worry about. He had a war going on, along with other operations Marines were involved in around the world. I thought to myself, he really didn't have the time or really wanted to hear about my problem. Besides who was I, nothing more than a Corporal in Vietnam. No one knew of this added mental pressure that was placed on me. I would have to deal with it. I continued to do my job. I was young and dumb. This was called getting the shaft or being stuck with the green weenie. In civilian terms, they call it "Getting Screwed!"

This was just another obstacle placed in front of me, but it would have a big effect on my Marine Corps career. Certainly, there was a degree hurt and emotional disappointment. The promotion was something that I really wanted, but it was not to be. Was it my section leader or someone else in the squadron that didn't want me to get the promotion? I would never know for sure. There was no bitterness, but there should have been. My personal moral was shot and at a low end. I did not have the time to worry about it. As a Crew Chief, I continued working on my chopper and flying on my assigned missions. I felt great being away from the base. It was just my chopper and flight crew. I was a member of the team and that was how I was treated. With the light of the morning sun, we took to the air with our passengers and cargo. I had my job to do.

Stabilization Augmentation System adjustment to YT-3 aboard the USS Valley Forge. S/Sgt. Jack Hiltibran in the green shirt.

LAST COMBAT MISSION

The first week of May 1968, we were flying near the Laotian border and assigned had to pick up a Recon Team. We couldn't land. The pilot held the chopper in a hover. I guided him in backing up the helicopter to the mountain. My chopper had come close to the tree tops with the aft rotor blades. I went to the ramp and pulled the team aboard, as I had done many times before. We dropped the team off back at their base. While we were flying, the sound of rotor blades just did not sound right to me. Over the whine of the engines and the popping sounds of the rotor blades biting into the air, you learn every sound and I knew that something was wrong. I told the pilots to land, which we did. We were sitting in a large clearing, in the middle of nowhere. Our wingman was flying overhead, covering us. I had the pilot to shut down the blades.

Upon checking the blades, I found that they had hit the tree tops and had cut open slits into several of the pockets along the rotor blades. This made a whistling sound that I heard. I took out my aluminum blade tape and knife. I quickly repaired the blades. My copilot wanted to know if the chopper was safe to fly. I told him that it was, as we all got in. We lifted back into the air and were off again heading back to the ship. If the rotor blades had hit a thicker part of the trees, the pilots would have lost control. We would have rolled down the side of the mountain, crashed and burned. Everyone would have certainly died. Little did I know, but this would be my last combat mission and another prayer was answered.

While we were flying back to the ship, the pilot stated there was a vibration in the aircraft. It was called a one per and he could feel it through the flight controls. I knew that it was a result of our hitting the trees. Something was out of alignment or out of balance. The helicopter is very sturdy, but also very fragile. There are a lot of moving parts that all have to work together. We arrived back aboard the carrier and the aircraft was downed for this vibration.

Standing on flight deck talking to pilot through the ICS cord aboard the USS Valley Forge

Now the maintenance began and I changed the damaged rotor blades. We went on a test flight and the vibration was still there. We came back and this time, I changed the rotor heads. I was working with the Technical Representative from Boeing Vertol, and we went on another test flight. The vibration was still there. We could not determine what the problem was. The third time, I took the drive train apart. I was putting it back together and had to go to the maintenance office. I glanced at the status board mounted on the wall of the aircraft in the squadron. My name was not by YT- 14, my chopper. There was no name on the board as the crew chief of this chopper. Someone had removed my name from the chopper, but why?

I contacted my section leader, who was a Sergeant. I asked him about what was going on. He told me that they had taken my chopper away from me, because I was incompetent. He said that I hadn't flown a combat mission in two weeks and my chopper was not in a flying status. I told him the chopper still had a vibration and it was not safe to fly. I was working with the Technical Representative from the Boeing Company. He could not find out what the problem was. If he couldn't figure out the problem, how was I supposed to find it? They were waiting for me to put the chopper back together again. Then they would take my chopper away from me. I never asked or found out who the "They" were. This was the biggest insult to me. I told my section leader that I was going to quit flying and turned in my flight equipment. My combat flying career was over.

I began working as a mechanic, while we were still on the carrier. I would have flown until my last day in-country, but I guess that it was not meant to be. It is one thing to work on an aircraft and another whole story when you are part of the flight crew. There is a certain pride about saying this chopper is mine. Yes, there was a degree of arrogance among the flight crews, but we earned it. I had been called many things in my life, but never incompetent. I just couldn't believe that he had actually called me incompetent. I knew the helicopter better than anyone did. I had to, by being on flight status. Flying is a sickness and I had it bad. I knew I was going to miss that feeling. I was grounded again, but this time the difference was that it was my choice.

I became a member of the Recovery Team. This group would respond to recover any chopper that was down in the field. Either it could be fixed and flown back or we stripped it for everything useful and then it was blown up. This assignment was voluntary and more than my regular job. As I think of it now, no recovery team responded when I was down in the field with the transmission trouble. I don't think we even had a recovery team at the time. The Federal Aviation Administration would have had fits knowing that we were using parts from a crashed chopper. They would have grounded every chopper in country. There was a big difference between military and civilian aviation. During most of the time in Vietnam, we were short on spare parts. Everything from low temperature grease to oil seals for the blades were in short supply. We would take helicopters and engines apart and use many of its parts. This was called cannibalization. We were not crazy, reckless or suicidal. We did our job, besides we had to fly in them. We did whatever it took to keep the choppers flying.

Around the end of May, my section leader came to me and stated that we had a chopper at Marble Mountain. It needed an engine changed and had to be brought back to the ship. He wanted me to go and get the chopper. I told him that I couldn't go. He asked why not and I replied, because I am incompetent! He said that we really need that chopper. I finally said I would go, and that was just to get away from the ship. He gave me two new guys that were fresh from the States. We loaded a quick change jet engine unit and tools onto a chopper. It lifted from the flight deck and flew to the base at Marble Mountain in the morning.

We got to the chopper and I checked it over. One of the new guys said to me, "Where's the book?" He was referring to the maintenance book for repairing the chopper. I began to laugh and told them that they were not in the States anymore and there was no book out here in the field. You have to know what to do. I showed them what to do and we changed the engine. I checked it over and called for two pilots. When the pilots arrived in the afternoon, they asked me if the Quality Control Inspector had checked my work and I said no. I say that it is flyable. The pilots trusted my word and besides, I was going to be flying in it with them. The other crew chiefs and pilots knew what my abilities were and they had faith in me and my judgement. That is all that mattered to me and what made a difference. We flew back to the ship.

One thing I could never understand, My Section Leader had told me that I was incompetent. He was the same one who had sent me to retrieve a downed chopper, with two rookies. Yet, I did not receive any training to improve my skills. I was working as a mechanic on the flight line. My Proficiency Marks were up, and I was teaching the new Marines in-country how to do their jobs. Other Marines asked me for advice on flight operations and mechanical problems with the choppers. The pilots trusted my judgement. But then again, I was incompetent. This statement hurts me to the bone, even all the way up to this very day.

Upon arriving back aboard the carrier, we learned there had been an accident. An Army chopper had tried to takeoff, while still being chained to the flight deck. The chopper flipped over, crashed and burned. The crew had been killed, including the Navy's flight director. This happened on spot number 1 at the front of the ship. There was a big black charred spot from the fire, where the accident had occurred. No one said working aboard the ship was easy or safe. Actually, the flight deck is a very dangerous place, with tractors on the move, rotor blades turning, jet exhaust, as well as choppers landing and taking off. There was always something going on. Jet fuel and ammunition were everywhere, not to mention falling overboard, were just a few things to worry about. There were many jobs that had to be performed correctly. The tension was always high. You could also die doing this work.

In June of 1968, we lost another helicopter. Our choppers were cleared into an area that we had been shelling with artillery. Well, somebody screwed up and an artillery shell hit our chopper. There was no explosion, but it knocked off a section of the rotor blade. The chopper came down out of control, crashing in a field. Three of the four crewmembers were killed. The copilot was medevaced. Chalk another one up to friendly fire. My chopper, YT- 14 went to overhaul and repair, for more extensive maintenance. More than a month of squadron level maintenance and it still had the vibration and had not flown another combat mission. I guess that it wasn't my fault for not finding the problem, because no one else could find it either.

Back in the States, Senator Robert Kennedy was running for President. Well, someone didn't want this to happen, and he was assassinated. It seemed as if you didn't like someone or what they stood for, the answer was to shoot them down. The Society back home was getting more and more violent and they called us killers. The anti-war protests were getting larger. These people didn't care about us or what we were going through. Society was not backing their troops. It was do your own thing, free love and drugs. They were enjoying life in America. This was not our way of life. We were living for our brothers, holding on to each other from day to day. Then again, we had more important things to worry about, like getting home alive.

There really wasn't a sense of time, while I was in-country. The sun came up and the sun went down. The days turned into weeks and the weeks turned into months. With each sunrise, I knew that it was one less day I would have to spend in Vietnam. There was wishful thinking about being back in the world, but no real plans. Life was short and we would not make any plans not knowing if we were going to make it home. I guess we were superstitious and we didn't want to tempt fate. We knew there was a life back in the States and we wanted to be a part of it.

REAL SHORT TIMER

Well, I was a short timer again, with less than ninety days left to do in-country. You start to get very nervous, but the countdown begins again. I had drunk my second bottle of Seagram VO and placed the second ribbon on the other side of my cover. This time I had to wait until we got off of the ship to celebrate. There was no booze on the ship. Now the thinking began, all that it would take is an accident, one mortar round, or rocket or a bullet to turn everything upside down. I could be dead or wounded, I guess that there was something to worry about. Before that, you couldn't worry about it and still did your job. Now you started to worry, but not to think about it.

We off loaded the ship back to the base at Marble Mountain. My time in-country was really getting short again. I was still working on the flight line. We were very close to the South China Sea. It was only a short stroll to the beach. The beach was beautiful with white sand. My swimming had not improved, but it was hot. You could walk out about 100 yards and the water was about five feet deep. A big storm was coming, so what did we do? - We went body surfing during the storm. The waves came crashing against the shore. As the wave came in, we would swim with it and get on the crest. We were body surfing and it was a new adventure. Well, we got onto the wave, but no one ever told us how to get off of the wave. We were flying on the waves and then it would dump you close to the beach. I had scrapes on my forehead and shoulders from hitting the beach, and I really do mean hitting the beach. Nobody said that we were smart. After the storm, the shore wasn't the same. I walked into the water and found myself going down hills. This came from the erosion from the waves hitting the beach. As I sank, the water covered my head. I sank like a rock, which was natural for me. It was like falling off the end of the earth. I got back to the surface and swam back to shore. That was it for me! I didn't come this far only to drown over here. I guess that it was getting too dangerous being over there or I was just thinking more about it now.

I knew that it was time to leave, when an Officer chewed me out for walking from the flight line with my shirt over my shoulder. I had finished working and it was hot. He told me that a Marine doesn't carry his shirt like that and for me to put it on, which I did. This is combat? He was fresh from the States and I knew it. One of the Veteran pilots or Officers would not have been so petty. This means only one thing to me, it was time to leave. Civilization had come to the War and it was time to go home. This would be my last duty station in Vietnam.

Being in Vietnam was very strange. We could not leave our base without a weapon and you could not get on the Air Force Base with a weapon. No weapons in a combat area, what a way to fight a war! We went to the Air Force Post Exchange at DaNang, they had everything there. There had to be at least four of us to go at a time. Two would go onto the base and buy things while the other two guarded the weapons. After that, we would swap positions and the other two would go onto the base. It was an all day affair. Those guys in the Air Force were living in two story air conditioned buildings. They even ate off of china plates with silverware. Now this is how you should fight a war. I think that they got hazardous duty pay, if the air conditioning went out. It seemed like everyone was living better than the Marines. Then again, you can't miss what you never had. Don't let me see what I have been missing.

It was July 1968, another Crew Chief, Cisco was shot in the hand, while flying on a mission and was medevaced. He was sent to Japan and back to the States. He was gone. We didn't see or hear from him again. We lost another chopper. This time it was Randy Little. He slept in the cot next to me and a very close friend. I looked at his cot with its blanket and pillow that he had neatly made. I would never see his face again. I thought of the fun and games that we had. He was as crazy as the rest of us, but this was too close to me. We had shared everything. We could talk about anything there or at our home. We dreamed about what we were going to do when we got home. Randy had begged my Mother in a letter, to send us a cake. Mom had made a cake, froze it for a week and sent it. When it arrived, it was still fresh and it was good. He then wrote back for her to send another cake, only with a bottle of booze in it the next time.

This day, Randy had gotten up and readied his chopper as usual. He and his chopper took off. There was nothing different about the day, except he did not come back. To this day, I still don't know what happened to his chopper. His chopper flipped over, crashed and burned. All that I know is that we lost an entire crew, along with their passengers, another pain of combat and four more friends lost. Their laughing and smiling faces were gone forever. No more sharing the fun and games of life. There was another very big void in my life and everyone in the squadron felt the same. It never gets any easier. The hurt of losing a friend and brother never goes away.

I was working on an aircraft as a mechanic on the flight line. We were removing a jet engine from one of the helicopters. The cable on the bomb hoist holding the engine broke and the engine fell. I was standing directly under the engine at this time. As it dropped, I pushed the rear of the engine up and the front end swung down. The front end of the 300 pound jet engine hit me in the back of my right leg, knocking me to the floor. The engine hit the floor of the chopper with a loud bang. A Major was walking by and he yelled at me saying, "Do you know how much that engine cost?" I did not answer him because if I did, I would have had my own court martial. I was taken to the first aid station for treatment of the abrasion to my leg. I was in pain and could not stand on my right foot. Seeing that I had less than a month left to do in Vietnam, I asked the Corpsman to place me on light duty status, for the rest of the time that I had to do in-country. This would give me a break from the long hours and hard work. He signed the papers. I returned to the hooch area and tried to relax. I learned to appreciate this time off.

In the middle of July 1968, YT- 14 came back from the overhaul and it was given to my first mechanic. He was now the Crew Chief of this chopper. He flew with this chopper for about a week. After one flight, he approached me and said that his cherry was broken. We walked over and looked at my old chopper. There it was a bullet hole. She had taken a bullet through the shaft that connects the two rotors. There was a big hole through the tunneling cover. No one was injured and she brought them home. YT- 14 had taken its first bullet and lost its' Cherry that day.

Throughout my entire time of flying in Vietnam, my chopper never took one hit by enemy fire. This was something that most flight crews couldn't say. I was CHERRY (a Virgin to being hit by enemy gunfire). I didn't say that they didn't shoot at me, because they certainly did. They never hit the chopper that I was in. I never heard the sounds of bullets popping as they were going through the metal skin of the chopper. When another Crew Chief would say to me that he was Cherry, I would reply, talk to me after you have been here for a while, like a year. I had flown on more than 320 combat missions, an untold number of sorties, along with more than 600 flight hours in combat. I had been awarded 16 Air Medals and my Combat Aircrew Wings. I was only down in the field twice, and both times were for mechanical problems; once with the transmission problem and once with a broken hydraulic line. There had been plenty of close calls, several hard landings, but no crashes. My chopper had hit some trees, but it had always brought us back safely. Many missions had been completed, along with many prayers that had been answered.

I had flown missions in some of the most dangerous battles and missions of the war. My chopper had flown through hails of bullets, along with surviving rocket and mortar attacks. The enemy didn't even scratch the paint on my chopper. This all goes back to my Mother and her praying. The power of prayer and her prayers kept me safe. I really think that her prayers kept me out of harms way. Combat will make you into a believer in a higher power. I had many Guardian Angels flying with me, because I was all over the place. Thanks for the prayers and the Angels that needed a much deserved rest. I can definitely say that — "God was my Co-Pilot" or at least a member of the crew. My Pilots and Copilots were definitely no Angels.

One of the Vietnamese workers told me that we were going to get hit that night. I had learned to believe them, because they knew what was happening. The only problem was that you never knew at what time we were going to get hit. So we sat around the hooch and waited, but there was nothing. I sat on my cot until about one in the morning. Nothing happened and everything was quiet. I told my friend that I was going to take my shower. I grabbed my towel and headed for the showers. I got into the shower, got all wetted down and lathered up. Wouldn't you know it, the sirens went off and the lights went out. I grabbed my towel, wrapped it around my waist and ran from the showers. There were loud explosions of rockets hitting the base.

I began to run toward the tent area with the safety of its bunkers. A couple of rockets impacted there, wrong way. I stopped, turned and began to run toward the flight line. These were the only places that there were bunkers. I ran up to the top of a sand dune, when the rockets began to fall along the flight line. I turned and again heading back for the tent area. I was slipping and sliding on the sand. At this time, I slipped and fell with the sound of the rockets was getting louder. They were walking the rockets right down the flight line and towards me. I began to roll down the sand dune, losing my towel. I stopped rolling and was lying on my back, looking at the sky. I held out my hands in anticipation of a rocket landing in them. At this point, I was tired of running and had just given up. The rockets stopped and the lights came back on. I walked back to the tent area, as the men came out of the bunkers and returned to their hooches. There was never an all clear signal. The rockets or mortar rounds just stopped falling.

I picked up my towel and walked into the front of my hooch. All of the guys began laughing. Some were rolling on the floor as I had walked in with my towel over my shoulder, bare foot, and naked. I was covered with soap and sand from the top of my head to the tips of my toes. I stood there for a couple of minutes and just shook my head from side to side. I then walked over to my cot, sat down and waited. I sat there until the sun came up before I went back to the showers and finished my shower. With my luck, we would have gotten hit again if I tried to take the shower any earlier. Well, it took me several days to get all of the sand out of my hair and ears.

I was really taking it easy with my injured leg. My section leader came to me in my hooch and said that he was going to get my light duty status taken away from me. He left and headed for the sickbay. I left and went to the squadron's office and came back to my tent. When my section leader came back, he said that I was to return to regular duty. I was to report to the flight line. I looked at him and smiled. Without saying a word, I simply handed him my check out papers and walked away from him. It was official, I was going home. I began packing and giving away things to those that were staying.

My last night in the squadron was nothing but a party. We got very drunk, but what else was new. I was with my friends, brothers forever. I never thought about not seeing them again, but there really wasn't the thought of leaving. It was our way of saying goodbye. There were no tears, just drinking, laughing and joking. We talked of stories of the many experiences, good and bad that we had shared. There were no goodbyes, but a lot of hugs. I was leaving my other family. We would never be together again like this as a squadron. I would never forget them.

There were no such things as a readjustment period, mental counseling or even a simple attitude adjustment session of what to expect, before returning to the World. No one cared about us, but us. It was a matter of clinging to each other for our own survival and sanity. We drank our beer and booze. We listened to our music and sang our songs. Whether it was soul music or even country and western, it did not make a difference. We learned and knew all of the words whether you liked them or not. It was a different kind of world, but it was our world.

I had spent a year and a half away from home and in combat. Throughout the entire time, there had been a lot of learning and maturing on my part. We had visited several countries and learned to respect people and their cultures. We all had a new outlook on life that wasn't taught in school. This was a true learning experience. When you leave the United States and see what the rest of the world has to offer, you can really appreciate the things and the lifestyle that are in this country called America. I wondered if life back home had changed or were things still the same. How would people look at me? These were just passing thoughts, because I would find out for myself.

The sun rose in the morning. I woke up and found myself curled up, lying in the corner of the tent. Mornings are rough, when you are still hung over from the night before. Everyone had gone to work and the war went on, as usual. The morning flights were still taking off and the maintenance had to be done. Pulling myself together, I got cleaned up. I hadn't really finished packing and the plane was not going to wait. I think that I left half of my stuff in my hooch, but I was out of there. It was my turn to leave and to go home. I wondered if anyone had ever missed their flight back to the world. I had arrived in Vietnam with the comfort of being surrounded with friends of an entire squadron. Now I had to deal with the solitude of going home alone. No matter what, it was August 2, 1968, and I was out of there and homeward bound.

GOING HOME - BACK TO THE WORLD

I was happy to be leaving this place called Vietnam. There was also a degree of sadness knowing that I was leaving my fellow Marines, my Brothers behind. We had fought, served and aged together. There is a brotherhood for those that have served together in battle. Those that have fought under our flag, the stars and stripes, have a sense of loyalty to each other that really can't be described. There is no doubt about our sense of duty and the respect that we had for each other. The squadron and each flight crew are made up of Officers and Enlisted Men. We were a team. We relied on each other. We depended upon each other. We loved each other. We lived, died and fought for each other. When in combat, there is no difference of being of different skin colors. Did everyone have these same feelings? I really don't know, but these were my feelings. We were all equal, Americans doing our jobs.

I believe there is no greater responsibility in life than that of being a Helicopter Crew Chief. Working on and flying in a helicopter gives you a feeling of pride and a sense of accomplishment that is beyond any comparison. Lifting off of the ground, with every flight the passengers, the flight crew, the cargo we carried, all depended upon your ability to perform your job effectively. Most people will never experience such devotion in their lifetime. There were eighteen pilots and crew members from our squadron had given their lives trying to accomplish the mission of supporting, protecting and caring for the Grunts, while I was in Vietnam with this squadron. The Marines that served with them will never forget their loss and sacrifice.

I left the MMAF and had made it to the big jet airliner in DaNang. It was bye, bye Vietnam. I must say that throughout it all, I believe that I had upheld the Tradition, Pride and Honor of the Marines. I did my job to the best of my ability and had earned the respect of my fellow Marines. My squadron, HMM-

164 was one of the finest helicopter squadrons in Vietnam. I was proud to have been a part of it. This meant more to me than anything else. I was leaving the tradition and the care of my brothers to my replacements. I was also saying goodbye to a lot of Vietnamese friends that I had made, during my time in their country. They would be left to continue the fighting and suffering. I was also saying goodbye to Mister Charlie. Yes, Charlie had earned my respect as a formidable foe and enemy.

The cabin door of the airliner closed. The plane was full of passengers. Everyone was very quiet, as we rolled down the taxiway. The plane sat at the end of the runway, waiting for our turn to take off. I think we were all holding our breaths. This was too close to going home to have something go wrong. We rolled faster and faster down the runway. There was a loud cheer that went up from everyone, as the wheels left the ground. We took off and headed into the sky. I think that there was a cheer on each and every plane leaving Vietnam. We had survived our tour of duty in Hell. It was now time to go home.

The plane landed in Okinawa, where we were processed. We were not allowed into the town but restricted to the base. The next day, we were driven back to the airport on buses. Here we were standing at the terminal, waiting for our turn to board the plane for home. With my luck, I was included with three other Marines as standbys. This meant that, if there was an emergency, we could get bumped off of this flight. We would be rescheduled on the next flight. The aircraft filled up fast. Sure enough, there were four Marines that had to go home and we were bumped from the flight. The four boarded the plane in our place and the door closed, leaving us standing there. The Marine standing next to me began to cry. We were this close to going home. I told him we would be on the next flight tomorrow. This didn't make a difference to him. He was crying like a baby, with the tears were flowing down his cheeks.

We were about fifty feet from the stairway leading up to the plane. We backed up and watched the big jet begin to taxi to the runway. As the big white jet plane took off heading into the bright blue sky, a tear began to roll down my face. The expectations and the excitement of leaving was too high. We were so close to going home, maybe too close and then to be told that you can't go. I think it was one of the saddest feelings that I ever had.

After a very long day and night, the next day came. We rode the bus back to the airport. We boarded the airliner, but still worried that we might get bumped again. We strapped into our seats, held our breaths and waited. The cabin door closed. There was no way that anyone was going to stop us this time. The jet plane rolled onto the runway and started to accelerate. As the wheels left the ground, there was a loud cheer from all of us. The plane was heading east over the Pacific Ocean. We were going home, back to the United States. We were heading back to the WORLD. I must admit that there were no thoughts of those that were still in Vietnam. I knew what they were doing, and my heart was there with them. This was the last big jump across the pond to the States. It was a long flight (not like going over there in short hops). This time with every minute, we were getting closer to home. The thoughts were of getting home and what we were going to do when we got there. My fellow Marines were still in Vietnam and were hoping to make this flight home. I prayed that they all would make this same trip home.

We landed at Travis Air Force Base in California. We had heard about the antiwar protesters, but there were none there or at least I didn't see any. I wanted to visit Lonnie's family, but I didn't think that they really wanted to see me. His death was still fresh in their minds, as it had only been six months. I think there would have been some closure for me too. There was always the question — Why am I coming home and Lonnie had to die? When I saw him last, in January, he was smiling and joking. Now he was gone and I missed my friend. His family might not have understood my feelings. Lonnie had been a member of my Marine Corps Family, and I loved him too. There were no goodbyes for us. I began to think back to Norman's funeral. I knew that I was not ready for those feelings to resurface. I would have to live with this pain and sadness. I didn't have the time to find out. My next flight was for Memphis, Tennessee taking off the next morning. After a couple of days with friends, it was off for New York. I was back home and there was a big sigh of relief from my parents. There was Mom's loving smile and warm hugs. Dad's Big Dummy was home and physically in one piece. He knew all about the mental pressures that can change your life, after being in combat. I would have to live with them, just like he did.

I would spend the next ten months assigned at the base in New River, North Carolina at the Air Facility, again. I was flying, training maintenance personnel and pilots in the combat operations of this chopper. We were doing the maintenance on the choppers as we did in combat, fast. We had to slow down to teach the new mechanics. There were Pilots, mechanics and Crew Chiefs stationed here that I had served with in HMM-262 and HMM-164 in Vietnam. This assignment made our transition back to living in the States much easier. I bought a car and was able to travel on the weekends. Life was good.

In the spring of 1969, there was going to be a wedding. Monty Pearson was from Georgia. He had met a very pretty New York debutante and had fallen in love. Monty was a Crew Chief and we had flown together in HMM-164. He had invited some of his Marine buddies to his wedding. About twenty of his fellow Marines made the trip for the weekend party. The wedding and reception were being held on Long Island in New York.

The wedding was beautiful and it was off to the reception that was being held at the Country Club in Port Washington. It was a warm day with a beautiful blue sky. It was a perfect day for the wedding couple. We drove up the long driveway and onto the beautifully manicured property. We had only read about this kind elegance and luxury of the American life. Did people actually live like this? Maybe this was just too much class for a bunch of combat veteran Marines.

Everything was fine, until we reached the front door of the clubhouse, where the reception was being held. I was stopped at the door and was told that I could not go in. I reached for and took out my invitation to show it to them. I was then told that I did not understand. Blacks were not allowed in the club. I was in a state of shock and dumbfounded. I felt like I had been stabbed in the back. Was this really America, the same country that I had fought for? This is the same country that my friends had died serving. Needless to say, I was the only Black person invited to the wedding and reception. After the Civil Rights Movement, Civil Rights Act and countless demonstrations things were still the same. I had seen and felt the pains segregation and discrimination in the South. This was not the Deep Dark South, but this was New York, right here in my own backyard. Who did these people think that they were, Americans?

I was upset because I couldn't get into the reception. Personally, I was mad and hurt all at the same time by the attitude of these people, but they would never know it. I was standing near the door, trying to think about how I was going to get into the reception. Several Marines came outside to see why I didn't come inside and what the problem was. I told the Marines what was said and they were not very happy. A few Marines went back inside the club, while some stayed with me. After several minutes, one of the Marines looked out of the front door. He waved to me to come on in. There were some disapproving stares at me by the managers and staff, as

I entered the building and walked into the ballroom. Nothing was said directly to me. The bride and groom arrived, along with the wedding party. We ate, danced, drank and really enjoyed the reception. We felt good and were glad for Monty. He was lucky and had found some happiness in his life.

After the weekend was over, I learned that the Marines had told the management they were going to tear the Country Club apart, if they didn't allow me in there. My fellow Marines, My Brothers had stood up for me. I was proud of them for taking this stand for me. Then again, why should they have to take a stand for me — I was an American, just like they were — or was I? The Constitution of the United States says that all men are created equal, but it does not say that all men are to be treated as equals. This was just another part of the learning process — being a Black Man in America — The Double Standard of living in this country.

On the day that I was discharged, there were promotions to the rank of Sergeant. Not for me, I was now the Senior Corporal in my squadron, 26 months in grade at the same rank, and with a Good Conduct Medal. Who said that life was fair. I knew that some MARINES thought that all MARINES were green. Then again, there were some that thought some Marines were a little darker green than others. I never did learn who it was that didn't like me. I would have stayed in, if I had received the promotion to Sergeant. I didn't get it and they didn't get me.

 It was June 16, 1969 and my military tour of duty was over. I was getting out of the Marine Corps and ready to start a new life. It had been raining all morning, but the sun came out as I drove out of the main gate and stopped. I looked back at the Marine Sentry at the main gate to the base. The bright sunlight sparkled off of the brass on his uniform. I felt very sad and began to wonder if I had made the right decision. My decision was made. Whether it was right or wrong and only time would tell. Talk about equality. Being in combat, life and death are equal. We lived to survive and we depended upon each other for our daily survival. I learned that being state side and in civilian life, it was not the same. There were two different worlds in this country and they were not equal for everyone. I was finished with one war and heading to fight the second one. I turned back around, looked at the highway and drove off the base. I was headed for home.

I knew that I was going to miss my Marine Brothers and the friendships that were formed under fire. The love and respect for each other cannot be matched anywhere else in life. I thought of those Marines that had died. They would never experience this feeling. I would never forget them and the moments that we shared. We had seen too much and done too much, but we were together. It was more than what the vast majority of society would ever experience. I guess that this was another part of the maturing factor of getting older and appreciating every precious moment of life. It still did not make the feeling of leaving my Marine Family any easier.

I wear my silver and gold Combat Aircrew Wings around my neck, in the memory of all those that served their country. When a person sees my wings and knows how they were earned, I don't have to explain anything else. I am a man that did his job in combat. My wings carry all the emotions and feelings, good and bad, of being in war. With all due respect to those that have earned their parachute wings, these wings were earned the hard, hard way and not by jumps in the USA. The memories are imprinted in my mind, along with periods of depression. The missing of the fun and games, the faces of those lost and those that survived, the thrills and the dangers, along with the excitement of being in combat will forever linger in my thoughts.

Every combat veteran will tell you that they were not a hero. They were just doing their job, just like me. We ride an emotional roller coaster of the experiences that we had lived through. There is no filling the void of having lost friends in combat. Those that had died are the true heroes. We honor those that made the supreme sacrifice as Heroes. They are the ones that will never get any older and are forever young. Their names are etched in the black panels on The Vietnam Memorial Wall in Washington, D.C. They will be remembered long after we are dead and gone.

LESSONS LEARNED

You can get discharged from the Marine Corps, but you can never take the Marine Corps training out of you. You can do anything that you set your mind to do. The word "can't" was taken out of my vocabulary by the Marines. I would learn this throughout the rest of my life and in everything that I did. There is a certain pride and honor that is instilled in you. You are somebody and there is something special about you. You walk a little taller and stand a little straighter. The public will never know the pain that is carried inside.

Nothing can prepare you for the sense of loss of fellow Marines in combat. Their faces, smiles and the memories shared are always in your mind. This is something that you have to learn to live with. Throughout each day and every year, there are good days and bad days, but those that were lost are never forgotten. We live with these memories every day and will grieve for them the rest of our lives. You are a Marine until the day you die and the fellowship will always be there. Society, as a whole, could really care less about the traumas carried by veterans. Veterans are separate but equal in the treatment that we received. The problem is the treatment was negative.

I was really heading back into the WORLD and it felt very strange. I had the same feelings of pain and confusion that every Black Military Veteran had felt coming home from every war, that they had ever served in. We had fought for our country and did our duty, but for what? I was re-entering a world of discrimination and of a double standard. Though some of the walls of segregation had been torn down, there was more unequal treatment to come. Dad had a saying, "The rules are the same for everyone, until it is your turn, then the rules change." This was another fact of life that I was learning.

There was a deep feeling of hurt thinking about how other Americans looked upon me. Questions were running through my mind. What did it take to be considered a man or even a human being? What does it take to be an American? What does it take to be treated as an American by other Americans? What does it take to be treated equally as an American? The White Veterans did not have these questions or problems. Their only problem was that of being respected as a veteran. This was the same problem that we all had to encounter and endure with society's attitude towards us. Our own country had turned its back on us. In my case, it was not only being a Vietnam Veteran, but as being a Black Man. Why was this allowed to happen?

It is very difficult to fight two wars with two enemies at the same time; One war against an enemy in a foreign land and the other was with your own country, with the enemy that didn't respect their fellow citizen as being an American. I had lived through one war. I was now heading back to fight the war of equality. I had fought for my country. Vietnam was a very unpopular war, but that didn't matter to us. We were not the politicians. We just did our duty. My friends served, and some had been killed and wounded. They were Americans, no matter where they were from or what color they were. Those that served with them respected them, no matter what race they might have been. Certainly there are Racists in the military, but there were no complaints when my chopper flew into a landing zone and they saw who the Crew Chief was. There were no overt color lines in Vietnam, just Americans doing their job. We did not fight for God and Country, but for our fellow Marines and under one flag — The American Flag.

Blacks have served this country throughout the course its history. I began to wonder where were the people of color? I know that they were there, but they not mentioned in the regular history books. It was like they were not even there. Their history was being passed on by word of mouth, from generation to generation. There is a lot to be proud of the accomplishments of those that were treated as less than an American Citizen. They fought and died, trying to uphold the honor and the sanctity of the freedoms of this country. They just wanted to be respected as being a man, an American and to have an equal chance, but it would not be that way.

During the Indian Battles of the 1870's, Black Army soldiers received their nickname of the Buffalo Soldiers, because of their dark skin and curly hair. In the Spanish American War, Buffalo Soldiers fought along side of Teddy Roosevelt in his charge up San Juan Hill. These soldiers also protected the southern borders of this country and had pursued Pancho Villa into Mexico. Throughout their battles, twenty-three Buffalo Soldiers were awarded the Congressional Medal of Honor, this country's highest honor for their bravery. It is very strange, they were not even treated as first class citizens, by the same citizens that they were protecting.

During World War One, Eugene Bullard went to France and joined the French Foreign Legion and was wounded. He later became a fighter pilot for the French, with the famed Lafayette Flying Corps. He was a Black American, who was born and raised in Georgia. He had painted on the side of his airplane these words, "We all bleed red " and flew 30 combat missions against the Germans. He was not allowed to fly or fight for the United States when they entered the war. He was a combat fighter pilot, so he had the ability and experience, but he was Black. He was honored by the French Government with numerous medals and awards and is considered to be a hero by the French people. He received nothing from this country, but a slap in the face.

The Harlem Hell Fighters were an all Black Infantry Regiment from the State of New York. When they arrived in France during World War One, they were given to the French, used French equipment, and were placed under French Military Command. Our White American Generals did not want them under their command. They were the first Americans to land in France. The Germans dropped pamphlets to these troops that asked this question, "Why would you fight for a country that treats you as less than a man?" The regiment fought with honor and had the distinguishable record of being in continuous combat longer than any other American fighting unit during this War. Not one soldier refused to fight and they never gave up one inch of ground to the enemy. This Unit received many French awards for their actions. In France, statutes were erected to their bravery. At the end of the war, they returned to the United States. Those that served in this regiment received nothing from this country, but years of degradation.

On the Sunday morning of December 7th, 1941, forces of Japan attacked the U. S. Naval Base located at Pearl Harbor in Hawaii. Aboard the battleship U.S.S. West Virginia was a Black Mess Steward by the name of Dorie Miller. His duties were to wait on and serve the Officers of the ship. During the attack, he took over a machine gun on the ship. Miller did not receive any formal training in the operation of this weapon. He began firing at the attacking Japanese aircraft diving at his ship. He is credited with shooting down three and some say as many as six of the enemy airplanes. Twenty eight enemy aircraft were shot down during the entire attack on the base. He was awarded the Navy Cross for his actions, that went above and beyond the call of duty and his duties. Why wasn't it the Congressional Medal of Honor?

The Black pilots known as, The Tuskegee Airmen of World War Two, had endured countless, untold types of discrimination and indignation throughout their service. The mistreatment was not only by civilians, but our own military Officers and Enlisted personnel. Their entire ground maintenance crew was all Black and they kept their airplanes flying. During their air combat, they never lost a bomber that they were escorting to an enemy aircraft. When the war was over, not one of these pilots could get a job flying with a major civilian airline company.

During World War Two, the Red Ball Express was a supply truck convoy driven mainly by Black Soldiers. They supported General Patton in his push across France. They drove day and night to provide the fuel, food and ammunition to sustain the attack against the Germans. There was also an all Black Tank Unit under Patton's command. Black Soldiers had also liberated a German concentration camp, saving a countless number of Jewish people's lives. Because of segregation, there was a naval destroyer, the U.S.S. Mason in the Atlantic Ocean, with an all Black crew that escorted convoys to Europe. All of these men did what was asked of them and they did their jobs. Why were these American Servicemen still being treated as less than second class citizens?

The Asian Americans were uprooted and placed in internment camps, during World War Two. This same treatment was not inflicted upon the vast majority of German and Italian Americans, where both of these countries had a number of spies and agents living here and actively working against this country. Asian American families were disrupted and their businesses destroyed. Their young men volunteered to fight for this country. Their country and home, namely this country was under attack, and they wanted to serve. They were sent mainly to Europe, where they distinguished themselves in combat. Years later, their families would receive some compensation for this country's mistreatment of them and their families.

The Native Americans and Blacks suffered the same, and sometimes even worse discriminatory practices from their fellow citizens. They have never even received an apology or any kind of compensation for the misdeeds inflicted upon them. They all fought bravely for a country that didn't treat them as equal citizens. In some cases, they even had to beg to fight for the land that they lived in, this country. They were not drafted, but volunteered. There were many more instances that occurred, but this history was not being taught in school.

It would take fifty years to award seven Black Soldiers the Congressional Medal of Honor, for their actions during World War II. Why did it take so long for them to be recognized? Why is the loyalty of American Minorities questioned? There were many more acts of bravery that have gone unrewarded. They know who they are and what they had done. Those that served with them know of their actions and many survived because of what they did. This history is being lost. The stories and the history of the double standard, mistreatment and injustices are now just being told.

Why doesn't Society teach the true history of this country? This country is now proud of its' military, which is now a true mixture of its citizenry. Before, we were looked down upon. Some people hoped that these untold stories would be forgotten. A lot of the deeds and events of Minorities in this country have been swept under the rug and in many cases, without even a word of thanks. Every segment of this society has always wanted to do their part to make this country great. To be an American, you should be proud of the contributions by all of its' people, because no one race of people can claim this country. The blood, sweat, tears and the lives of all of those that lived here, established the United States.

The World knows about the millions of Jewish people that were killed in Germany during the Holocaust of World War Two. What about the approximately 55,000 men, women and children that were Black Germans? They lived in the Rhineland region of Germany. What happened to them? Nothing is ever mentioned about their deaths or the sterilization experiments that took place under Hitler's regime. The hatred of Blacks by Nazi Germany was also demonstrated and documented by the deliberate execution of Black Prisoners of War.

No one ever talks about the thousands and thousands of Black Africans that were taken from their homes as slaves that died during the Middle Passage to this country. The sick and dying were simply thrown overboard into the Atlantic Ocean to die. The exact number will never be known. Taking nothing away from those that died, but there was also a Black family aboard the Titanic. A Black man fought and died at the Alamo, along with Mexican Americans. There is nothing ever said about these parts of history, but they did happen.

Certainly many questions have been raised, along with very few answers. Why is the involvement of Blacks and those of color in this country's history being suppressed? Blacks also had to fight for their own human dignity. This world history is also not being taught or even talked about. As there is only one true history of this country, there is only one true history of the world. The history is not perfect, but it is good and bad. It should be told.

After World War Two, the United States Armed Services were desegregated. The rest of society would take another decade to feel this same thing. Court cases, riots, sit- ins, demonstrations, full public knowledge and the awareness of what was going on in this country would be needed to improve life in this country. It would take the United States Supreme Court, along with federal troops to try to rectify some of the past wrong doings of this society. Lawsuits and the Civil Rights Act would also be needed, ten years later. There is still more work to be done to make this country a land of true equal opportunity.

In July 1980 my father, Milton H. Beamon, Sr., passed away. Years later I received his high school yearbook and at the bottom of his picture were the following sentences, **"Staking his ambition high — to be President of the United States — "Slim" has intentions of joining the Marines before taking over the chief executive's position. At present math and**

English have more appeal than political speech making, but he expects to enter the field of politics soon."

These were bold words from a Black Man graduating from Leavenworth High School in Waterbury, Connecticut in 1942. His class was the first to graduate after the Day of Infamy, December 7th. This was the time of segregation, discrimination, unequal treatment, and denied equal opportunities in this country. There were no Blacks in the Marine Corps at this time and very, very few Black Politicians. Dad had his own aspirations and he dared to dream. After graduating from high school, he was drafted into the Army during World War II. He served in the Quartermaster Corps in Europe. I believe that he was just born too soon. I would have voted for him to be President. He had never mentioned this fact to any of us. I wish that he had. His inspirations were instilled in us as he guided us, while we were growing up.

At the bottom of my high school yearbook picture it says, "I am going to be a Marine". Times had certainly changed. I think Dad might have thought that I was living his dream of being a Marine. During the 1960's, my father got one of my brothers interested in politics. My brother, Reggie was later elected as a State Legislator to the House of Representatives for the State of Connecticut. Dad had died before this happened, but his legacy and dream continues to live on.

No, this country is not perfect and neither are its citizens. There have been many miscarriages of justice, in the long history of this country. It saddens me by the conduct of those in the past and present for the treatment given to their fellow citizens, but I am not bitter. Most people came to this country in a boat, not all in the same type of boat. Well, we all are in the same boat now. This boat is called the United States of America. This is my country and it is my home.

We remember the past, to live today and to make tomorrow better. We will make tomorrow better for all of its' citizens. A new generation of Americans was emerging, and we would make our world better than what it was. We would settle for nothing less than equality. A Vietnam Veteran or any other combat veteran knows and understands more about the meaning of equality and freedom, than what the rest of society will ever know. If you are good enough to fight and die beside me, then you are good enough to live and work next to me.

If Rosa Parks is considered to be the Mother of the Civil Rights Movement, then the Combat Veteran is the Father. The vast majority of society did not have such an intense educational lesson. Americans would still have to learn about what it means to be an American. Why do some of the best, the brightest and most intelligent men and women of this country have to die serving it? They were protecting everyone's rights and freedoms that live in this country. No one has more of a right to what this country has to offer than the ones that had fought for it. The draft dodger, war protestor, college student, deferred student, drug addict and alcoholic, all sat here in relative safety and all looked down on the Vietnam Veteran when they returned home. It is shameful for this type of attitude for those that were serving their country. Most of this Society does not appreciate what it means to be an American, but they enjoy the pleasures and freedoms of this country. They have never paid their dues. Freedom is not free. The Military Veterans of this country have paid the price for all our freedoms, in peacetime and in time of war. This lesson is not being taught in a classroom, but has to be learned.

MY MARINE HELICOPTER FAMILY —
HMM-164

In April of 1990, I attended the first reunion of HMM-164. I had left the squadron in 1968. We were meeting in Washington, D.C., which was appropriate. While driving down the highway, I thought to myself that maybe I should leave it all in the past. The war was over. Then I thought that there might be some closure for me and I wanted to see the Brothers that I had left behind. Upon arriving at the hotel, there was a sign over the registration desk stating, "Welcome HMM-164 Association." There were signs and the employees were wearing buttons saying, "Thank You Vietnam Vets". This was the first time that anyone had ever said thanks to us for our service to our country. It seemed a little strange after all of these years. After registering, I made my way to the conference rooms and there I found former Marines from 1966 to 1970. This was the entire time the squadron had served in Vietnam. This unit had been the first CH-46 squadron in country and had suffered the last two deaths during Operation Frequent Wind in April 1975. This was the evacuation of Saigon at the end of the war in South Vietnam.

About 125 Marines attended this reunion. Luckily, there were about 30 from my era, Pilots and Crew Chiefs alike. It was like an old home week, a real family reunion. After all the years, the family had come together. We shook hands and hugged each other. We learned and healed from each other. There were no feelings of having to explain anything. No matter what year we served in Vietnam, we had experienced the same pressures, fears and pain. The feeling was that of — Been There — Done That — I Understand. Nothing else was needed to be said. We were not demented veterans, as Society had labeled us, but useful members of the Society. These men were pilots, doctors, lawyers, businessmen, policemen, firemen, and the average working man. We had melted back into Society, living our lives and raising our families as best as we could. We did not care what Society thought of us or of the war. We were a true Band of Brothers. Wives and girlfriends stated that this meeting should have taken place 20 years earlier. They were starting to understand the emotions that we had been carrying inside throughout the years.

There I saw Mark "Worm" McDonald, who had survived his flight attempting to rescue the Breaker Patrol. Gary Horton had survived his crash in the water, at the waterfalls at base of Khe Sanh. There stood Ray "Ready" Rothenberger, Jerry "Jelly" Jellison, Tom Kennedy, Paul "Weird" Mountain, Duane Douglas, Bill Crews, and more. They were all my fellow Crew Chiefs, my brothers. Officers and pilots were also there; "Smedes" Butler, Steve Fetzer, Bernie McGinley, Dick Rosser, Colonel "Dad" Watson and Bill "Ole Dog" Weaver, to name a few. I had flown as part of a flight crew or wing man with all of these people. The memories of flights and missions came flowing back, as if they had happened yesterday. It felt good being with my other family. We were all older. Some of the guys had put on weight, others had lost their hair, while others hair was grey. We were not as lean and not as mean, but we were all still Marines.

The squadron members that were present of HMM-164, along the family members of some of those that had died (including the Parents, widow and daughter of Capt. Looney) slowly assembled. We held a very solemn ceremony, as a Marine Bagpiper played on the grassy knoll to the right of the Vietnam Memorial Wall, in the bright blue skies and warm spring sunshine. The visitors to the Memorial were stopped from entering the walkway, to allow us complete access. We marched slowly down to the path entering the Memorial Wall. A wreath was placed at the center of the Wall by two of our Commanding Officers. A flower was placed in front of each black panel with the name of those that had died from our squadron. This was our Vietnam Memorial for those that had given their lives. The Wall is a piece of each and every person that served in Vietnam. There were many tears shed for our fallen Heroes. The Marine Corps Barracks in Washington provided a firing squad, a bagpiper, and a bugler, who played "TAPS", in honor of our fallen squadron mates. This was my first trip to the Wall and I would not have wanted it any other way.

To go to the Wall, with those you had served in combat and to pay our respects to those that will never get any older, was not only a privilege, but an honor. Our comrades were gone. They were missed, but not forgotten. I know that if my name was on the Wall, they would have done the same for me. The families of those that had died were welcomed into our helicopter family with open arms. We that served with their sons, as brothers, also shared their loss.

Vietnam Memorial Flyover

We left the Wall and returned to the hotel, needless to say, we were all emotionally drained. There was still more to come. We were staying on the side of the hotel talking about the day's event, when we heard an unmistakable sound. We all looked up and there it was. We looked in awe as a CH- 46

Helicopter was coming straight for us. It circled the hotel in the clear blue sky and landed within a hundred feet of us. Everything was fine and everyone was cheering and smiling, until the chopper shut down the rotor blades. The air was filled with the smell of the JP-4 jet fuel, which brought back all of the memories of Vietnam, in an instant. We cried for those that had died, those that were not there and we cried for each other. The tears flowed like a river and there wasn't a dry eye. Nothing had to be said — It had meant only one thing — I Understand. This Marine chopper was flown to the reunion on the orders of one of our pilots. A hundred and one stories of old missions were told by the old salts. The young flight crew understood, as we crawled all over their chopper, inside and out.

This was the first reunion and it was the best. There would be many more reunions to come, but nothing like this one. It was a weekend that no one wanted to end. We left and returned to our homes in many different States around the country. My Marine Helicopter Family was alive and well. We had made it home. They loved me and most of all, respected me. I loved them all.

In July 1996, I attended a Popasmoke Reunion (USMC/ VIETNAM HELICOPTER PILOTS AND CREWMEMBERS ASSOCIATION) in Las Vegas. There were more faces that I hadn't seen in almost 30 years. I was reunited with Mike Botch. He was also a Crew Chief in HMM-164. We had flown through the major battles together. We lived in the same hooch and had dove into the same bunkers. I had not seen him since 1968. His home was in Pennsylvania and that was where I was looking for him. When I first saw him, he had his back turned to me and I recognized him right away. I walked up to him and said, "You are still as short as ever." He turned around, smiled, and we hugged. It was like seeing a long lost brother. We walked down the hot streets of Vegas and talked about what had transpired over the years, since we had last seen each other. We spoke of our families, jobs and life being back in the World.

Mike was working for a major airline in Texas and I told him that I was a cop. There was a sudden state of shock on his face. I told him that I never got caught. We both laughed. I then told him that I was the first Black Lieutenant in the history of the City of Waterbury. He looked at me strangely and said, "What's this Black Shit!" I returned his stare. He said he never looked at me as being Black. I then apologized to him, because I never looked at him as being White. There wasn't any color division in Vietnam amongst the flight crews. We were Americans and most of all, Marines protecting and caring for each other. I had succumbed to one of the evils of this society, separating ourselves by color. Nobody had given me this rank. I had earned it. I was a Police Lieutenant and in charge of the Juvenile Division, that is all. Thank you, Mike for putting me back in my place; standing tall, side by side, next to my brother.

Years later, I was at a Veterans' Day Ceremony in November on the Green in Waterbury. A tall White man and his wife approached me. He looked at me and stated, "You were in helicopters in Vietnam!" I replied, "Yes, I was." He said that he had been in the Marines. He then said to me, "You medevaced me in April 1967." I looked at him strangely and said, "To be honest, I really don't know." He then said, "You were flying at the Battle of the Hills?" I replied, "Yes, I was." He said, "Then, it was you!" We had medevaced a lot of Marines from that Battle. He said that he had been shot in the neck. I truly didn't recognize him. He would have been covered with dirt, mud, bandages and blood. How could I remember him after such a short flight? Only he knows for sure, whether or not it was me. I was in a state of shock. He identified himself as Joe O'Neill and introduced his wife. We hugged and welcomed each other back to the world. Joe had been awarded the

Bronze Star and Purple Heart Medals for his actions, during the Battle of the Hills.

What are the odds of two Marines, not knowing each other, from the same hometown, being in Vietnam at the same time, in the same place, with the number of Marines and helicopters there, to be medevaced, to return to that same hometown and his remembering the Crew Chief on the chopper that brought him off of that hill and to the hospital for treatment, after more than 30 years?

Well, I guess that I had won the lottery with these odds, just by seeing the smile on his face. It is not very often that you get to see a person of whose life you saved. I was just doing my job, but I get a warm feeling all over every time I see him. Joe O'Neill had made it all worthwhile. This is what it means to be an American. Through his eyes, he respected me as a man, a fellow American and a fellow Marine. I had this same feeling with the members of the squadrons. This feeling was also missing in civilian life, because of the double standard, but Joe was a fellow Marine. I am a Black Man living between civilian life and the love of those in combat. The feeling of being accepted and respected as being a human being and a Man was all that I was ever looking for.

I am not really into labels for people and I really don't like being called an African American. The same also goes for those called Irish American, German American, Italian American and so on. There is nothing wrong with remembering, respecting and honoring your ancestry, but we live in the United States of America. This means that you are an American FIRST, and this Heritage comes FIRST. I am an American first - An American of African decent. I know what my ethnicity is and the history behind it. The same should be for every other group of people in a country that is called the melting pot. I am an American. The rest of the world looks at us this way, why can't we look at each other the same way? As Martin Luther King, Jr. stated,

"One day a man will be judged by the content of his character and not by the color of his skin." One day, this might be true in this country. Maybe I am just dreaming or is it just wishful thinking?

I don't mind being called a "**MARINE**". This is not a label, but a title. It is an honor and I am very proud of it. I had earned this title, as did every **MARINE** that has served the Corps with **HONOR**. Every time the Marines' Hymn is played, there is a sense of pride and a tingling sensation that comes over me. These feelings come from the tradition, memories, experiences of being in combat, witnessing countless acts of bravery, and my being a part of history. The loss of our fellow Marines was not in vain. They gave their lives trying to help their fellow Americans to survive. For those that served with them, their sacrifice will never be forgotten.

These were some of my memories of being a Marine, a Helicopter Crew Chief and a Combat Veteran. The memories were good, bad and indifferent, but they mean everything to me. At this time of my life these memories have helped to mold me into the person that I am today. I will always carry those bitter sweet thoughts, the emotions of war, and of being an American with me every day. They are moments in time of being in combat, and the pressures of being in a place called Vietnam, but the feelings are the same for anyone that takes to the air in a helicopter in combat. The memories also raised the questions of equality that will someday be answered. What does it take to be considered an American? These are the memories of a man who happens to be an American of African, French and American Indian decent. I am a Marine, a very proud person of whom I am and what I have accomplished and experienced.

Life is a learning experience, but it is also precious, fragile and very short. It should be cherished. Nobody can promise you tomorrow and whatever you decide to do in life — be the very best that you can be. Whenever I recite the Pledge of Allegiance to the flag, I believe in every word that is said especially, "One Nation under God, with Liberty and Justice for all." I will do my best to make every word come true. Nobody said that life was going to be fair or easy, but I will try to make it as fair as possible.

The struggle for equality continues!

The slogan, **"ONCE A MARINE ALWAYS A MARINE"** - is not only a saying ---- but is also a **FACT**.

SEMPER   FIDELIS

ALWAYS   FAITHFUL

HEROES OF HMM-164

FEBRUARY 1967 TO AUGUST 1968

**The Marines that I served with and made
The Ultimate Sacrifice in Vietnam.**

Capt. Paul T. Looney	Killed In Action	May 10, 1967
Capt. Gary T. Porter	Lost At Sea	June 20, 1967
L/Cpl. Leslie E. Englehart	Lost At Sea	June 20, 1967
L/Cpl. Earnest R. Byars	Killed In Action	July 30, 1967
L/Cpl. Robert L. Biscailuz	Killed In Action	July 30, 1967
1st Lt. Craig H. Waterman	Killed In Action	July 30, 1967
Capt. David A. Frederick	Killed In Action	July 30, 1967
Cpl. Thomas A. Gopp	Killed In Action	August 3, 1967
L/Cpl. Harold Bauchiero	Killed In Action	August 20, 1967
Cpl. Lonnie W. Clark	Killed In Action	Feb. 23, 1968
Cpl. Gary L. Columbo	Lost At Sea	March 6, 1968
1st Lt. Glenn J. Zamorski	Killed In Action	June 11, 1968
Sgt. Raymond W. Templeton	Killed In Action	June 11, 1968
Cpl. Conrad Lerman	Killed In Action	June 11, 1968
Capt. James L. M. Littler III	Killed In Action	July 3, 1968
1st Lt. Raymond C. Daley	Killed In Action	July 3, 1968
Cpl. Randell B. Little	Killed In Action	July 3, 1968
S/Sgt. John C. Bilenski	Killed In Action	July 3, 1968

There were more losses that I didn't know from the squadron, before and after I served in HMM-164.

More Heroes on The Wall:

Cpl. Dennis Richard Tabor	Killed In Action	June 11, 1966
Cpl. Robert Walter Golden	Killed In Action	June 11, 1966
Capt. Phillip Allen Ducat	Killed In Action	Sept. 25, 1966
1st Lt. Thomas Lee Burton	Lost At Sea	Mar. 1, 1969
Capt. William Craig Nystul	Lost At Sea	April 29, 1975
1st Lt. Michael John Shea	Lost At Sea	April 29, 1975

All of these Marines will never grow old
and will never be forgotten.

Printed in the United States
118508LV00005B/214/A